STUDIES IN COMPARATIVE AESTHETICS

Eliot Deutsch

Lewis Rowell

MONOGRAPH NO. 2 OF THE

SOCIETY FOR ASIAN AND COMPARATIVE PHILOSOPHY

THE UNIVERSITY PRESS OF HAWAII

1975

Copyright © 1975 by The University Press of Hawaii

All rights reserved

Manufactured in the United States of America

Library of Congress Cataloging in Publication Data

Deutsch, Eliot.
   Studies in comparative aesthetics.

   (Monograph of the Society for Asian and Comparative Philosophy ; no. 2)
   Bibliography: p.
   1. Aesthetics, Comparative--Addresses, essays, lectures. 2. Experience--Addresses, essays, lectures. I. Title. II. Series: Society for Asian and Comparative Philosophy. Monograph of the Society for Asian and Comparative Philosophy ; no. 2.
BH85.D48   111.8'5   74-34028
ISBN 0-8248-0365-5

STUDIES IN COMPARATIVE AESTHETICS

For Judy and Larry, Susan and David

the author

Eliot Deutsch is Professor of Philosophy at the University of Hawaii and Editor of the international quarterly *Philosophy East and West*. He is the author of *The Bhagavad Gītā*; translated with introduction and critical essays (1968); *Advaita Vedānta: A Philosophical Reconstruction* (1969), paperback edition (1973); *Humanity and Divinity: An Essay in Comparative Metaphysics* (1970), and (with J. A. B. van Buitenen) *A Source Book of Advaita Vedānta* (1971).

CONTENTS

List of Illustrations viii

Preface ix

CHAPTER

   I.   REFLECTIONS ON SOME ASPECTS OF
        THE THEORY OF RASA   1

  II.   AN INVITATION TO CONTEMPLATION:
        THE ROCK GARDEN OF RYŌANJI AND
        THE CONCEPT OF YŪGEN   24

 III.   BRUEGEL AND MA YÜAN: A
        PHILOSOPHICAL INQUIRY INTO THE
        POSSIBILITIES OF COMPARATIVE
        CRITICISM   36

CONCLUSIONS   84

BIBLIOGRAPHY   87

LIST OF ILLUSTRATIONS

The Rock Garden of Ryōanji 24
Bare Willows and Distant Mountains 37
The Massacre of the Innocents. 38

PREFACE

Aesthetics ought to be a disciplined reflection upon art-works and our experience of them as the art-works have their being in their own splendid vitality. Aesthetics ought thus to be unpretentious. Comparative aesthetics--the analysis, interpretation, reconstruction and evaluation of the distinctive aesthetic concepts and experience of cultures other than one's own--makes clear the need for aesthetics to be unpretentious, and it enriches, I believe, the possibility of aesthetics fulfilling its task of understanding the work of art in the fullness of its own being and our experience of it. Let me explain.

The art world is utterly pluralistic; which is to say, it is constituted by created works whose distinctive characteristic is precisely their uniqueness. Nothing is more striking philosophically about works of art than their peculiar individuality or personality. Each art-work, if it is successful as a work of art, is a world. It is a place of concentrated meaning and value. The members of other classes of objects in our experience, including ourselves, are, to be sure, individual; but the individuality does not have the kind of uniqueness that defines the class itself. The manner in which a work of art presents meaning in form in its own special way is just what makes it count as a work of art. This is not to say, though, that there ought not to be a distinction in function between the art critic and the aesthetician. It is indeed the critic who is concerned primarily with the aesthetic quality (and other relevant aesthetic dimensions) of individual works of art. Criticism is normative. Aesthetics is theoretical: it is a "field" of philosophy. The aesthetician, as a philosopher, needs nevertheless to be aware--and to be keenly aware--of the constitution of the art world, for otherwise he may fall victim to constructing a system in aesthetics which while alleging to be universal may be only a substitute for, rather than a means of insight into, art-works and our experience of them.

Aesthetic theory has often been pretentious. It has claimed, implicitly if not always explicitly, not to be bound by its own historical placement and to be applicable to art-works wherever they are to be found. But the big theories about what art is-- "communication," "expression," "imitation," "revelation" and so on--are, from anything like a multicultural or even historical intra-cultural viewpoint, tied closely to certain particular kinds of art and to a limited aesthetic experience. The big theories do have something important to say about certain particular kinds of art--some works of art do primarily <u>express</u> the artist's emotions; some works of art do essentially <u>communicate</u> ideas and values; some works of art do <u>reveal</u> aspects of being, of human life, of nature; some works of art do <u>imitate</u>, and others <u>represent</u>, human events and natural processes--but none of the theories properly apply to the art world as such. Each theory has to do with a <u>possibility</u> of art, but not, as they have often claimed, to do with "Art." This is especially evident when the arts of non-western cultures are included in the art world (a not unreasonable request). An intimate contact with at least some of these arts should compel the universalist aesthetician to rethink some of his most cherished concepts, notions--and assumptions.

Comparative aesthetics, I believe, ought to be carried out not with the intention of transplanting exotic ideas or with the expectation (or even desire) that these ideas will have an immediate and appropriate application in one's own culture; but rather with the hope that through the study and creative reconstruction of other cultural ideas, ideals and preferences we may enrich the possibility of our understanding philosophically the nature of art and aesthetic experience. Comparative aesthetics, in short, as with comparative philosophy generally, ought to serve philosophy itself.

. . .

In the following <u>Studies in Comparative Aesthetics</u> I have selected three rather large topics, with several themes, each of which is related to the thought and experience of an Asian culture.

"Reflections on Some Aspects of the Theory of <u>rasa</u>" discusses the problem of the subjectivity and objectivity of aesthetic experience. It also deals with the question of "expression" in art by asking, by way of the classical Indian theory, what it means to express an impersonal or generalized emotion; and with the problem of the qualifications that are necessary for the experiencer of the art-work to reach the art-work in its own unique being. Through the concept of <u>śāntarasa</u> the "peaceful state" to which art-works are said to point, the problem of distinguishing aesthetic experience from pure spiritual or religious experience is taken up.

In "An Invitation to Contemplation: The Rock Garden of Ryōanji and the Concept of <u>yūgen</u>" I try, on the basis of a "phenomenology" of the experience of the famous garden and an analysis of the writings of Zeami, the principal author of the Japanese Nō theatre, to explicate the concept of yūgen and to see what relevance the concept might have for a general understanding of aesthetic experience and the nature of beauty.

"Pieter Bruegel and Ma Yüan: A Philosophic Inquiry into the Possibilities of Comparative Criticism" addresses itself primarily to the question of what kind and quality of knowledge do we need to have of an art-work from another culture if we are to experience the art-work in its full aesthetic potential. By way of a comparative analysis of works by the sixteenth-century Dutch painter Pieter Bruegel and the thirteenth-century, Chinese artist Ma Yüan, and of the concepts employed by the traditional Chinese critic, I distinguish four dimensions of aesthetic relevance and examine each of them in terms of the primary problem. The comparative analysis seeks to make possible the drawing of distinctions in a significant way between an art-work and an icon and between subject-matter and content in art. It further addresses itself to the problem of whether there are universal principles of aesthetic rightness in art, and it tries, through an analysis of symbolism, to articulate the essential structures of meaning in an art-work.

. . .

I wish to express my appreciation to the National Endowment for the Humanities for the generous support given me by a senior fellowship award in 1973-74. Without the leisure for travel, study and writing afforded by that grant, this work would not have been possible. I also want to thank Kenneth Inada, president of the Society for Asian and Comparative Philosophy for the encouragement he offered toward the publication of this work. He has, through his thoughtful leadership, been largely responsible for the monograph series of the Society and for many of its other activities. David T. Wieck, Edwin Gerow and Henry Rosemont were kind enough to make many helpful comments and suggestions and I have benifited much from their expertise. I am also indebted to Floris Sakamoto for the care and graciousness with which she prepared the manuscript for the Press.

Eliot Deutsch
November 1974

REFLECTIONS ON SOME ASPECTS OF THE THEORY OF RASA

Indian aesthetics, it is often said, consists fundamentally of the theory of rasa--the term rasa being variously translated as "flavor," "desire," "beauty;" that which is "tasted" in art.[1] I want to reflect on rasa not simply in the mode of exposition and interpretation, but in the spirit of seeking philosophical understanding; which is to say, I want to know what truth there is in (at least some aspects of) the rasa-theory, and a truth, if such there be, which is not confined to traditional Indian drama, poetry or music. I want, in other words, to examine rasa not as a culture-bound (and probably descriptive) concept, but as a potentially universal (and possibly prescriptive) concept in aesthetics--East and West.[2]

I

Where is rasa located? Is aesthetic experience essentially a discernment of qualities belonging to the object, the art-work, or is aesthetic experience essentially a special response of the experiencer, of the subject to the object? This question, which is so enduring in much of Western aesthetics, with the differing answers giving rise to (or at least being closely associated with) theories about art as "expression," as "communication," as "objectified pleasure" and the like, was raised by the writers on the <u>rasa</u>-theory and was summarily dismissed by Abhinavagupta. He writes:

> The Rasa does not lie in the actor. But where then?
> ...Rasa is not limited by any difference of space, time and knowing subject.[3]

And:

> When we say that '<u>rasas</u> are perceived (we are using language loosely). . . for <u>rasa</u> is the process of perception (<u>pratīyamāna eva hi rasaḥ</u>) itself....[4]

J. A. Honeywell then properly notes that:

> It [<u>rasa</u>] is not an objective entity which exists independently of the experience as the object experienced; the existence of <u>rasa</u> and the experience of <u>rasa</u> are identical. The object of poetic experience is the poem, but nothing in the poem can be pointed out as its <u>rasa</u>.[5]

The essential quality of aesthetic experience, it is maintained, is neither subjective nor objective; it neither belongs to the art-work nor to the experiencer of it; rather it is the process of aesthetic perception itself, which defies spatial designation, that constitutes <u>rasa</u>. This view that the locus or <u>āśraya</u>, as it were, of <u>rasa</u> is nowhere, that <u>rasa</u> transcends spatial-temporal determinations, is, I believe, the only way open to us to understand the nature of aesthetic experience.

When we think of experience exclusively as experience _of_ some thing or other in the other's bare reality or objective giveness, we run the danger of assuming that we need only be attentive and open (passively available, as it were) to what is there and the object will disclose itself fully to us and satisfy our interest in it--as though sense-mental experience can at that level of consciousness be shorn of all the interpretive categories of the experiencer. In aesthetics this "objectivist" attitude leads to a one-sided formalistic concern that often sees aesthetic value only in configurations of lines and shapes, in abstract movements and the like (Clive Bell) and that tends to think of creativity in formulae-making or rule-following terms.

On the other hand, when we think of experience (as perhaps most of us do) as it is entirely a matter of _our_ response to some thing or other, as _our_ feeling or emotion, we are disposed to rob the world of its values and to assume, in a narrow and ego-centered way, that our own precious feelings and moods constitute the world. We believe then that every thing and every one is basically an _occasion_ for our experience; which leads us to further believe that experience is a matter of (indifferent) causes yielding (valuable) effects. In art and aesthetics this way of thinking leads to a one-sided romanticism, which finds nothing of value except in what may be located in a wayward subjectivity, and to gross sentimentality, where everything about the object may be reduced to and lost in titillating feelings or emotional paroxysms. Here we no longer experience the art-work but only ourselves.

The <u>rasa</u>-theory suggests that we can avoid these and other less extreme forms of spatializing aesthetic experience (and thereby misunderstanding it) if we understand aesthetic experience as a special process wherein the art-work <u>controls</u> rather than causes the response of the experiencer, and wherein the experiencer must also bring a highly developed understanding, sensitivity, and life history to bear on the work. To understand aesthetic experience in this way requires that we also understand that the content of art is never (or at least <u>ought</u> never to be) just the personal emotions or thoughts of either the artist or the experiencer. M. Hiriyanna rightfully points out that "the poet's own feeling, according to the Rasa view, is <u>never</u> the theme of poetry."[6] And that:

> As a result of their idealised character, art objects lose their appeal to the egoistic or practical self and appear the same to all . . . . They become impersonal in their

appeal, and therefore enjoyable in and for themselves.[7]

It is precisely this impersonality (sādhāraṇikaraṇa) or trans-personality of aesthetic content which enables the art-work to serve as a bearer of meaning and the experiencer to rise to a heightened consciousness of his self and the world. "Meaning" requires a sharing or a shared experience; and this sharing is achieved in art only when there is an intense impersonality, an impersonality which, paradoxically because of its intensity, is at the same time highly individual. This is the case for aesthetic experience because aesthetic interest, in contrast to mere practical interest, is given not to the individual *qua* individual, but to the individual as it embodies, becomes, represents, expresses--whatever you will--a universal, *inter*-personal--and thereby--transcendent quality.

This transcendental or extraordinary (alaukika) dimension of *rasa* does then (but rightfully) impose a great task upon the artist.

> The *rasa* is a generalized emotion, that is, one from which all elements of particular consciousness are expunged: such as the time of the artistic event, the preoccupations of the witness (audience), the specific or individuating qualities of the play or novel itself: place and character chiefly. Portrayal of the events within the work,

and characterization are thus the most delicate issues before the writer; inadequate portrayal--persistence of elements of particular consciousness--amounts to an obstacle.[8]

Art is a kind of <u>mimesis</u> according to the <u>rasa</u>-theory; but it is an "imitation" of a very special kind, for <u>rasa</u> does not imitate things and actions in their particularity, in their actuality, but rather in their universality, their potentiality--and this "imitation" is said to be more real than any particular real thing. The theory would agree, then, with Aristotle that history has the task of relating what actually happens, while poetry (art) of what may happen; that history records the activities of particular things and beings, while art expresses the possibilities of man and nature, and the gods.

A generalized emotion, the <u>rasa</u> as expressive of universality, is not to be confounded, however, with a mere abstract or utterly dispassionate state of being. To depersonalize in art does not mean to destroy personality, but to allow for its transformation: it means to attain to a passional-cognitive state that is nevertheless spiritual in character. How is this possible?

II

According to the psychology underlying the <u>rasa</u>-theory experience is an awakening or manifestation of various innate states (bhāvas or sthāyibhāvas) which exist in the mind (or "heart") as latent impressions (saṁskāras or vāsanās) that derive from one's past experience. Eight of these potential emotional states are distinguished: (1) pleasure or delight (rati), (2) laughter or humor (hāsa), (3) sorrow or pain (śôka), (4) anger (krodha), (5) heroism or courage (utsāha), (6) fear (bhaya), (7) disgust (jugupsā) and (8) wonder (vismaya). These states, in their essential characteristics, are the same for everyone, coming as they do from a common human life-experience. In actual life each bhāva is said to be accompanied by causes (kāraṇa), which are understood to be the various situations and events of life that occasion an appropriate response; by effects (kārya), the various visible responses (gestures, facial reactions); and by concomitant elements (sahakārin), various accompanying but temporary mental states such as anxiety.

> Every human being is born with a set of inherited instinctual propensities. His thoughts, actions, and experiences constantly generate impressions which sink back into the subconscious mind ready to be revived on the conscious level. These impressions, which are called saṃskāras [or vāsanās] in Indian philosophy and psychology, are organized around emotions. The emotions are related to typical and universal situations

and generate definable patterns of action.
. . . Apart from these clearly organized
basic emotions there are innumerable transit
feelings and moods which accompany the former
in any experience. . . . Anxiety, exultation,
bashfulness, languor, etc., are examples.[9]

According to the <u>rasa</u>-theory when these elements or dimensions of ordinary experience become elements or features of art and aesthetic experience they are called respectively determinants (<u>vibhāva</u>), the emotional situation that is presented in the drama; consequents (<u>anubhāva</u>), the physical changes or movements that signify emotional states; and transitory states (<u>vyabhicāribhāva</u>), the transient emotions that properly accompany various basic states. Abhinavagupta writes:

> Rasa, in this connexion, is just that
> reality (<u>artha</u>) by which the determinants,
> the consequents and the transitory feelings
> after having reached a perfect combination
> (<u>samyag yoga</u>), relation (<u>sambandha</u>), conspiration (<u>aikāgrya</u>)--where they will be in
> turn in a leading or subordinate position--
> in the mind of the spectator, make the
> matter of a gustation consisting of a form
> of consciousness free of obstacles and
> different from the ordinary ones. This Rasa
> differs from the permanent feelings [<u>bhāva</u>],
> consists solely in this state of gustation
> and is not an objective thing (<u>siddhasvabhāva</u>)....[10]

The <u>rasa</u> differs from a permanent feeling state, the <u>bhāva</u> or <u>sthāyibhāva</u>,[11] but is then correlated with it in the theory.

> Such expressions as 'the permanent sentiment becomes Rasa', are due to the correspondence (<u>aucitya</u>) only. This correspondence, to specify, is due to the fact that the very same things which were previously considered to be causes, etc., related to a given permanent sentiment, now serve to realize the gustation, and are thus presented in the form of determinants, etc.[12]

The "correspondence," then, between the permanent feeling states and <u>rasa</u> produces the basic <u>rasas:</u> (1) the erotic (<u>śrṅgāra</u>), (2) the comic (<u>hāsya</u>), (3) the pathetic or compassionate (<u>karuṇa</u>), (4) the furious (<u>raudra</u>), (5) the heroic or valorous (<u>vīra</u>), (6) the terrible (<u>bhayānaka</u>), (7) the odious (<u>bībhatsa</u>), and (8) the marvelous (<u>adbhuta</u>). To this standard list Abhinava, perhaps following some earlier writers whose works are not available,[13] added a ninth, <u>śānta</u>, or "the peaceful," <u>rasa</u>.

Now apart from the many subtle intricacies in this description of how a <u>rasa</u> arises the important issue for aesthetics, it seems to me, is the manner in which the <u>rasa</u>-theory ties <u>rasa</u> to the patterns of life-experience and sees the <u>rasa</u> as a kind of radical transformation of the ordinary into the extraordinary (<u>alaukila</u>). The theory enables one to relate art to life in an intimate way and at the same time to grasp their essential differences. G. B. Mohan Thampi discusses the theory in these terms:

> The characters and situations depicted in a poem have unique ontological status and our perception of them is <u>sui generis</u>. The special mode in which the poetic characters exist and are apprehended is indicated by the term <u>alaukika</u>, non-ordinary. In life our reactions to persons and objects can be described in terms of attraction, repulsion, or indifference. . . . Our responses are governed by positive or negative interests. Our attitudes of attraction, repulsion and indifference are put aside or transcended when we contemplate a character like Hamlet.
>
> . . .
>
> In poetic experience emotions do stir and agitate our mind; but they do not move out in the form of action. Further, in poetic experiences the emotional states are not simply undergone or suffered; they are perceived and tasted.[14]

Aesthetic experience, therefore, is essentially a "relishing" of certain generalized emotions which are "objectified" in a vital form. Art is at once bound to life and <u>is</u> for itself. A work of art that occasions <u>rasa</u> is closely related to common experience, drawing as it does its own vitality, its aesthetic content, from those basic life emotions and situations that persons everywhere endure. Form in art has meaning only in relation to content; in fact, there is a form, the <u>rasa</u>-theory suggests, only when for both the artist and the "spectator" there is a lived, deeply felt content. But a work of art is not a mirror of life; it is, once again, <u>alaukika</u>, extraordinary. It is <u>for itself</u>; which is to say, its content is uniquely aesthetic: it is there for apprehension, contemplation, participation; it is just there for sensitive understanding.

Aesthetic experience, according to the theory, is thus not something that is merely given, a fortuitous happening; it is an attainment, an accomplishment. "The tasting of Rasa," Abhinava writes, "...differs from both memory, inference and any form of ordinary self-consciousness."[15] It requires a like-heartedness on the part of the experiencer and the overcoming of a number of formidable obstacles.

III

T. M. P. Mahadevan has pointed out that "the poet uses words in a way which involves a process of impersonalising, and his poem gains the power of equal appeal to all. The reader who could enjoy the poem is a <u>sa-hṛdaya</u>, 'one of similar heart'."[16] Abhinava defines the <u>sahṛdaya</u> in his <u>Locana</u> as follows:

> Those people who are capable of

> identifying with the subject matter,
> as the mirror of their hearts has been
> polished through constant repetition and
> study of poetry, and who sympathetically
> respond in their own hearts....[17]

The ideal experiencer of art for the <u>rasa</u> theory is therefore not simply a passive <u>spectator of</u> but is an active <u>participant in</u> the work. As Hiriyanna states, the participant's "insight into the nature of poetry is, in point of depth, next only to that of the poet."[18] The realization of <u>rasa</u> thus makes rather extraordinary demands on the experiencer as well as on the artist.

> ...Rasa is, in any case, simply and solely
> a mental state which is the matter of
> cognition on the part of a perception
> without obstacles and consisting in a
> relish.[19]

Among the obstacles to the realization of <u>rasa</u> (which actually become demands made upon the experiencer-participant) that Abhinava distinguishes are:[20] (1) The lack of verisimilitude. We might consider this to be a failing more of the art-work and artist than of the experiencer of it, but Abhinava speaks of the obstacle as belonging essentially to the experiencer. "Indeed, if one considers the things presented as lacking in verisimilitude, he cannot obviously immerse (<u>viniviś</u>) his consciousness in them . . . ."[21] He then goes on to say that "the means by which it is eliminated is the consent of the heart. . . ."[22]

One of the conditions for aesthetic experience, for being a <u>sahṛdaya</u>, is that we be open to the art-work precisely as it is an art-work that is capable of controlling our experience of it. The "consent of the heart" means a kind of self-surrender to the object, an affirmation of its being capable of sustaining our interest and attention. Most persons, most often, glance at art-works and receive in return only a fleeting impression (what the work is "about," who the artist is). The <u>sahṛdaya</u>, the one of similar heart, must be capable of and must exhibit a power of unselfconscious attentiveness in order that he may relish the <u>rasa</u> that is to arise.

(2) Another of the obstacles that Abhinava refers to is just this personal attachment to emotions. It is "the immersion in temporal and spatial determinations perceived as exclusively one's own or exclusively those of another."[23] It consists, he maintains, "in the appearance of other forms of consciousness, due variously to the fear of being abandoned by the sensations of pleasure, etc., to concern for their preservation. . . ."[24]

This "obstacle" is rather obscurely presented, but the overcoming of it is central to the realization of the <u>rasa</u> as distinguished from the appropriate bhāva. Abhinavagupta is arguing here that the subject, the participant-experiencer, must universalize his own emotion by getting beyond the temporal-spatial specificity of his own immediate state of consciousness as this may be grounded in ego-needs and as it is bound to particular life-experiences. He must do this for the sake of recognizing the universalized emotion in the art-work, <u>as it is given only in the work</u>.[25]

The sahṛdaya, according to Abhinava, must be equal to the art-work; that is to say, he must be prepared to experience it properly. This may sound obvious: however, it is indeed the case, and it is often supported by aesthetic theories of an "art is communication" and "art is expression" variety, that most persons view aesthetic experience as a kind of therapy--of their bringing to an art-work a distraught consciousness for repair. It might very well be the case that experience of art yields a higher integration of self and a better ordered consciousness, but this is not something just produced by the art-work as though by some kind of causal efficacy; rather it is as well an achievement of the experiencer in his relation to a cooperating work.

Plato taught that "the fairest music is that which delights the best and best educated, and especially that which delights the one man who is preeminent in virtue and education."[26] The Platonic judge and the sahṛdaya are alike in this, they represent the "aristocratic" ideal of taste. But who else if not the one who is like-minded with the genius of the poet is best able to judge, to appreciate, to comprehend the poem?

IV

Rasa, we have seen, is neither subjective nor objective. It may nevertheless be analyzed with emphasis given to the subject, the participant-experiencer (as we have done with the origination of the rasa in terms of the bhāvas, the requirements of being a sahṛdaya, etc.) or to the object, the actual art-work. J. A. Honeywell explains nicely that

> Rasa, which is the end of poetry in terms of process, becomes in terms of poetry as an object the organizing principle which determines the unity and wholeness of the composition. Seen in this way, it can be used to distinguish the major parts of the composition in terms of their functions within the whole . . . .[27]

And further:

> Although rasa exists as an experience of a certain kind, it cannot be disassociated from the poetic object. The idea of rasa rests on the assumption that the poetic object is fully realized only in the experience of the compe-

tent reader. Rasa thus pertains to the experience of an audience in the presence of a poetic work and fully absorbed in that work. As such, the analysis of rasa is inseparable from an analysis of the poetic object. The properties of rasa must emerge as the actualization in experience of the properties of the object itself.[28]

Kant thought that the judgment of taste was entirely subjective, and yet necessary; that aesthetic judgments are compelling for the experiencer but that this doesn't require the determination of the properties or structure of the object. But Kant was wrong, and the rasa-theory is right; for one of the factors which clearly distinguish an art-work as a structured-content from a mere collection or aggregate of elements is the manner in which a feeling-tone suffices the work and gives unity to it. And if it is the case, as Susanne K. Langer maintains, that "Art is the creation of forms symbolic of human feeling,"[29] then that feeling-tone which unifies the work must at the same time be grounded in the deepest categorical structures of feeling; it must be transpersonal and universal; it must, in short, be the rasa.

Feeling awakens feeling: a universalized mental state can be apprehended in aesthetic experience only if it is constitutive of the art-work itself. The art-work as a whole becomes a vibhāva:

it determines the experience. "To determine," it must be stated again, is different than "to cause." Cause-effect relationships, as we ordinarily understand them in the context of human experience, suggest an indifference and independence between the terms, which separation simply does not hold for art and aesthetic experience. And this is especially the case when the art-work is capable, through the creative imagination (pratibhā) of the artist, of awakening in one who is prepared for it that special ecstatic unity of self and object wherein both achieve a completion of their being.

V

This brings us to our final consideration of the rasa-theory; the concept of śāntarasa as put forward by Abhinavagupta and the opportunity this concept affords for distinguishing between aesthetic experience and what we might call pure spiritual experience.

Śāntarasa, according to Abhinava, is just that transcendental realization of unity that is joyful and peace-ful. It is grounded in the Self and is realized as a kind of self-liberation.

> ...the Ātman alone possessed of such pure qualities as knowledge, bliss, etc. . . . is the sthāyibhāva of śānta.[30]
> 'Śānta rasa is to be known as that which arises from a desire to secure the liberation of the

Self, which leads to a knowledge of the Truth, and is connected with the property of highest happiness.'[31]

Śānta is silence. What is silence in art? A work of art is constantly speaking, as it were, and yet it is mute, standing silently in its own concentrated being. The painting, the poem, the play is a center of silence and requires for its right apprehension an inner quietude, a silencing of desires and thoughts. Silence in art is not empty, like a container into which one might put anything, rather the art-work that is right for itself participates in a silence which is the profoundest truth of being, the silence which is a dynamic harmony of all being and becoming.

Silence in art, then, is not a mere absence of sound. Śāntarasa is a plenitude; it is surcharged with creative energy. The silence calls us out of ourselves to the concentrated being of the work itself.

And herein lies the essential difference between aesthetic experience in its highest form and pure spiritual experience: the art-work calls our attention to it and controls our experience with it; the experience is temporal (albeit transforming); in spiritual experience the call is from that which is Real without division or object or time. The art-work, in the fullness of its experience as śāntarasa, points to Reality and participates in it. In pure spiritual experience there is only the Real.

To the enlightened--but only to the enlightened--all experience is śāntarasa.

Notes

1. The term rasa has had a long and varied use in Indian thought. As G. B. Mohan Thampi points out: "The dictionary records, among others, the following meanings: Sap, juice, water, liquor, milk, nectar, poison, mercury, taste, savor, prime or finest part of anything, flavor, relish, love, desire, beauty. The meanings range from the alcoholic [?hallucinatory] soma-juice to the Metaphysical Absolute--the Brahman. In different periods new meanings evolved out of earlier ones and in different disciplines rasa acquired different connotations." "'Rasa' as Aesthetic Experience," The Journal of Aesthetics and Art Criticism, XXIV, no. 1, part I (Fall 1965), p. 75.

2. I do not, of course, want just to ignore or set aside the historical development of the rasa-theory. It is important to recognize the different formulations of the theory from Bharata (2nd-5th Centuries?) in the Nāṭyaśāstra, through such thinkers as Daṇḍin (7th century) to Ānandavardhana in his Dhvanyāloka (9th century) and Abhinavagupta (10th century) in his Abhinavabhāratī, a commentary on the Nāṭyaśāstra, and his commentary, Locana, on the Dhvanyāloka, and to other later thinkers such as Viśvanātha (14th century). For purposes of this paper I will work primarily from the position of Abhinavagupta. His formulation of the theory is generally considered to be the most philosophically interesting.

It is also important, I think, to recognize the close relations that did obtain between the theory and the traditional arts of India, especially drama.

The theory was formulated first with respect to aesthetic problems connected with drama: once formulated the rasa-theory was then applied to, and refined in relation to, a rich variety of art forms. With a characteristic passion for classification and correspondences early Indian thinkers about music even correlated each single note of the octave with a specific rasa. See A. A. Bake, "The Aesthetics of Indian Music," The British Journal of Aesthetics, Vol. 4, 1964, pp. 47 ff.

    3. Abhinavabhāratī. See Raniero Gnoli, The Aesthetic Experience according to Abhinavagupta, 2nd edition (Varanasi: Chowkhamba Sanskrit Series Office, 1968), p. xxxvi.

    4. Abhinavagupta, Locana on Dhvanyāloka, in Śāntarasa and Abhinavagupta's Philosophy of Aesthetics, by J. L. Masson and M. V. Patwardhan (Poona: Bhandarkar Oriental Research Institute, 1969), p. 73.

    5. J. A. Honeywell, "The Poetic Theory of Viśvanatha," The Journal of Aesthetics and Art Criticism, XXVIII, no. 2 (Winter 1969), p. 168.

    6. M. Hiriyanna, Art Experience (Mysore: Kavyalaya Publishers, 1954), p. 34.

    7. Ibid., p. 31.

    8. Edwin Gerow, "The Persistence of Classical Aesthetic Categories in Contemporary Indian Literature" (unpublished paper).

    9. G. B. Mohan Thampi, op. cit., p. 76.

   10. Abhinavabhāratī, in Gnoli, op. cit., p. 78.

   11. In personal correspondence with the author Edwin Gerow has rightly pointed out that if we follow the implications of Abhinava's arguments we should "take the rasa as the bhāva from which the elements of particular consciousness (time, place,

etc.) have been expunged. There is no cause and effect relation because the rasa is what is really there, and has been there; but in 'normal' experience, it is determined by the accidents of our daily and personal awareness, rather than in and of itself. This 'other-realization' is the peculiar capacity of the play, as instrument--but it creates nothing new--it simply reveals."

    12. Abhinavabhāratī, in Gnoli, op. cit., pp. 80-81.

    13. See Edwin Gerow and Ashok Aklujkar, "On Śānta Rasa in Sanskrit Poetics," Journal of the American Oriental Society, Vol. 92, no. 1 (Jan.-March, 1972), p. 81.

    14. G. B. Mohan Thampi, op. cit., pp. 76 and 77.

    15. Abhinavabhāratī, in Gnoli, op. cit., p. 81.

    16. T. M. P. Mahadevan, The Philosophy of Beauty (Bombay: Bharatiya Vidya Bhavan, 1969), pp. 39-40.

    17. Abhinavabhāratī, in Masson and Patwardham, op. cit., p. 78n4.

    18. M. Hiriyanna, op. cit., p. 41.

    19. Abhinavabhāratī, in Gnoli, op. cit., p. 62.

    20. Abhinava distinguishes seven obstacles in all, but the list is a rather curious one insofar as it includes elements which would appear to be taken account of entirely in terms of the art-work itself, and it includes a factor ("having the right means of perception") which is not so much an obstacle as simply a necessary condition for experience. Ibid., p. 67.

    21. Ibid., p. 63.
    22. Ibid.
    23. Ibid., p. 62.

24. Ibid., p. 64.

25. Abhinava recognizes of course that it is largely up to the artist to aid in overcoming this obstacle. "The means of eliminating this obstacle," he writes, "are the so-called theatrical conventions (nāṭyadharmī), which include a number of things not to be found in ordinary life...." (Ibid., p. 65).

26. *Laws*, 659a, trans. by B. Jowett.

27. J. A. Honeywell, *op. cit.*, p. 166.

28. Ibid., p. 169.

29. Cf. *Feeling and Form* (New York: Charles Scribner's Sons, 1953).

30. *Abhinavabhāratī*, in Masson and Patwardhan, p. 131.

31. Ibid., p. 139.

The Rock Garden of Ryōanji

AN INVITATION TO CONTEMPLATION: THE ROCK GARDEN OF RYŌANJI AND THE CONCEPT OF <u>YŪGEN</u>

I

A garden of just stone and gravel, a piece of physical nature, and yet it invites one to participate in contemplative being.

The old wall enclosing the rear of the garden is heaped with time; the rocks too are weathered by time, but the garden is timeless. The garden engenders meditation; but not upon itself so much as upon the depth and utter quiescence of being.

The Rock Garden of Ryōanji in Kyoto is at once precise and natural. There is nothing "romantic" here, there is no restless, self-conscious yearning for transcendence; neither is there anything "classical" here, no effort is made to embody some perfect, abstract ideal. The garden is complete, but it is not "finished." It is simply an invitation to contemplative being.

The Rock Garden suggests this paradox, that the juxtaposition of elements which constitute it is at once arbitrary and necessary. One can imagine that the elements could be changed and exchanged without doing violence to the quality of the whole. It would be a different work, in a "surface" sense, yet one feels that its invitation would be the same.

26

Yet it is precisely the present arrangement of elements which offers the invitation.

The garden is not asymmetrical insofar as asymmetry implies symmetry as its standard or measure. The garden is not asymmetrical and it is not symmetrical; it is irregular in just that unique way which comes from the splendid fusion of chance and determination.

One cannot imagine being in the garden, or that a child belongs there digging and building. As a work of art it cannot properly be used.

One cannot apprehend a garden in the same manner as a painting or a piece of sculpture, for a garden makes available too many perspectives. (The fifteen stones of the Rock Garden cannot, in fact, be grasped all at once from any horizontal perspective.) One can stand in front of a painting from many positions, but it is the "same" painting that one sees in a stronger sense than when seeing a garden from different locations. It is as if the garden contained a multiplicity of perspectives in potentia. But wherever one sits on the bare deck that faces the garden one gets the same invitation.

The Rock Garden demands our inwardness; it compels us to still our mind, to look beneath the relentless flow of image, idea, and desire; it tells us that we will find neither an abyss from which we must flee nor a radiant splendor that will enrapture us: beyond that it tells us no more. It is an invitation to contemplation.

Unlike most works of art, no amount of familiarity with this Zen Rock Garden can provide one with any very solid assurance as to what it is that one will meet when experiencing it; for the work drives one into oneself. One can, to be sure, be rather certain that the formal disposition of elements, and the elements themselves, will be much as one left them when one was there before, but one cannot anticipate the quality of the new experience. The work, in other words, does not lead one through a determined set of responses, as does a novel or a symphony. The Rock Garden of Ryōanji is not a finished thing: it manifests yūgen and is thus an open invitation to contemplative being.

II

According to Zeami (1363-1443), who perfected the Nō theatre in its classic form and brought it to its highest level,[1] "Yūgen is considered to be the mark of supreme attainment in all of the arts and accomplishments."[2] It has been pointed out, therefore, that

The aesthetic ideals which pervaded the poetry,

drama, painting, gardens, tea ceremony, and most other aesthetic activities during this [medieval] period were summarized largely in the concept of yūgen.[3]

And what a (conceptually) difficult, but (ontologically) simple concept yūgen is! Leonard Pronko gives us some sense of its elusiveness when writing:

> The difficult term yūgen, suggested by the stylized beauty of the mask and the spiritual reality behind it, has been translated in many different ways; indeed it is difficult to pin down, for Zeami used it with different meanings over a period of thirty-six years. The primary meaning of yūgen is the 'occult,' or as Waley translates it, 'what lies beneath the surface'. Other meanings are . . . transcendental phantasm, fathonless sentiment, transcendental insight, elegance, gracefulness, the subtle, the hint. . . . Yūgen results in beauty of many kinds: physical grace, elegance, quietness, and the like.[4]

Yūgen has also been defined as charme subtil ("Je précise que ce n'est pas là une traduction exacte de yûgen: cette interprétation m'a été suggérée par le contexte, et confirmée par mon expérience personnelle du nô."[5]); as that "supreme form of beauty. . . which is the ultimate goal and the essential element of all aesthetic experience;"[6] and as "the beauty not merely of appearance but of the spirit; it is inner beauty manifesting itself outwards."[7] "The term yūgen," we are told, with no surprise, "has no exact equivalent in English; literally it means 'obscure and dark,' but, as used by Zeami, it carries the connotations of half-revealed or suggested beauty, at once elusive and meaningful, tinged with wistful sadness."[8]

With specific reference to the Nō, Zeami maintains that yūgen is

<u>displayed in the performance</u>

> ". . . a display of yūgen in the Nō is apparent to the eye, and it is the one thing which audiences most admire,

<u>and is possessed by only some actors</u>.

> "but actors who possess yūgen are few and far between.

<u>Its essence is beauty and gentleness</u>.

> ". . . the essence of yūgen lies in a true state of beauty and gentleness.

<u>It is present in personal appearance as well as in art</u>,

> "Tranquillity and elegance make for yūgen in personal appearance.

<u>and especially in the speech of the "upper classes"</u>.

> "In the same way, the yūgen of discourse lies in a grace of language and a complete mastery of the speech of the nobility and gentry. . . .

<u>Nevertheless it is universal</u>.

> ". . . Whatever part he [the master actor] may be playing yūgen will never be absent. Whether the character he portrays be of high or low

birth, man or woman, priest, peasant, rustic, beggar, or outcast, he should think of each of them as crowned with a wreath of flowers. Although their positions in society differ, the fact that they can all appreciate the beauty of flowers makes flowers of them all.

It is a realm that the artist must enter.

"Unless an actor enters the realm of yūgen he will not attain the highest achievements.

And not through instruction alone, but by his "working out the principles" for himself.

"It is when the actor himself has worked out these principles and made himself their master that he may be said to have entered the realm of yūgen."

III

What, for aesthetics in general, have we to learn about beauty and aesthetic experience from the Rock Garden of Ryōanji and the concept of yūgen?

First, however, we have to acknowledge that in Western aesthetics, which began and developed as the theory of the beautiful, concern with beauty--be it elusive and profound, possessed by the artist and manifest in his work, or not--is no longer fashionable. In many ways this is not to be regretted, as this concern in the past so often was exhibited merely as a search for the essential qualities that supposedly made objects beautiful, with (from another point of view) the idea of beauty itself being just a function of a certain (at times rather precious) "aesthetic emotion." Not infrequently, in theory and practice, "beauty" became highly artificial.

But there have been regrettable consequences of this rejection of beauty in aesthetics and in art (in favor of an emphasis on "novelty," "expressive force" and the like), for the rejection has tended to trivialize art ("there is nothing mysterious about art;" "everyone is an artist") and to deprive art of much of its spiritual playfulness and joy.

The realization of yūgen in art calls precisely for a highly disciplined openness--an ekstasis, a playful "stepping out"--on the part of both artist and experiencer.

Yūgen is silence. It is that being of the artwork which, like śāntarasa, is, and participates in, truth of being.

Yūgen in art is that which informs a structured-content so that it becomes a radiant form. Whenever there is beauty in art there is aliveness and splendor.

Yūgen is at once entirely natural and wholly spiritual. It expresses what the particular work of art should be according to its own aim as an artwork, and to be apprehended it calls on our part for that intense and disinterested consciousness which we call "spirit."

"Consider any work of art," writes Raymond Bayer, "whose magic is potent: our soul steeped in it, does not pass through unchanged: one might even say that therein lies the authentic nobility, the criterion of the aesthetic object."[9]

The concept of yūgen teaches us that in aesthetic experience it is not that "I see the work of art," but that by "seeing" the "I" is transformed. It is not that "I enter into the work," but that by "entering" the "I" is altered in the intensity of a pristine immediacy. Is this magic?

What does it mean to be transformed by a work of art?

It is often suggested that a work of art represents a "harmonization of conflict," that an art-work integrates the raw contents of existential conflicts into a formed unity, and that the viewer, catharsis-wise, is able to recognize the structure of his own conflicts in the light of this unity and to receive thereby the impetus to order those conflicts and thus attain to the harmony to which the work of art, through its ordering, points.

But aesthetic experience, as we have seen with the theory of rasa, is not therapy. Works of art are not made simply to heal the divisions within the viewer. To experience a work of art properly one must be _equal_ to the work. One might initially be overpowered by the garden of Ryōanji, especially when one encounters it as a mere _stepping away_ from the humdrum chaos of one's ordinary being and routine, but if one is to be anything more than just overpowered, one must become as the art-work itself is--in truth of being.

Yūgen is objective--but in this very special way; it is there only when there is no subject as such to perceive it. For _yūgen_, for beauty, _esse est non percipi_ by someone as a quality of something; it is recognized only with the absence of the self-centered self or subject. To contemplate _yūgen_, then, means to apprehend for oneself, as oneself, the essential life of the art-work.

Beauty, the concept of _yūgen_ teaches us, is the _presence_ of the object as it is in truth of being. Beauty in art is thus thoroughly paradoxical in this, that it gives rise to the qualities by which it is apprehended; it becomes the essential being of that which it is thought to qualify.

What this means, in less dramatic language, is that beauty in art is not a quality among qualities; it is not something that is superadded to materiality; it is not properly a qualifying adjective which may give rise to a class of "beautiful things." Beauty in art is rather the art-work itself as a radiant form. I don't perceive the art-work as beautiful; I perceive beauty as the art-work.

"Aesthetic judgments," writes Harold Osborne, "are reducible in their simplest form to the proposition-type 'This thing is beautiful' or 'This is a beautiful thing'."[10] But, the concept of yūgen teaches us, they are not so reducible. Grammatically "beauty" might be a property, predicate or attribute; but then this is a mistake of grammar insofar as, ontologically, beauty is the very thing which it purportedly qualifies in that thing's own realized or presentative state of being.

In sum: The Rock Garden of Ryōanji presents itself as just the thing it is--rocks and gravel, in yūgen; in beauty that is at once radiant and abysmal. Yūgen informs the work and is the work in its own concentrated being.

Beauty, then, is not so much a quality of a thing as it is the thing itself as a presence to be apprehended in loving joy.

Notes

1. Zeami and his father, Kwannami Kiyotsuyu (1333-1384), are usually credited with the "invention" of Nō--the most disciplined and subtle form of theatre in Japan, and perhaps in the world. For good introductions to Nō and Zeami's contributions, see Donald Keene, editor, 20 Plays of the Nō Theatre (New York and London: Columbia University Press, 1970); Arthur Waley, The Nō Plays of Japan (New York: Grove Press, 1957), originally published in 1920; Japanese Classics Translation Committee, Nippon Gakujutsu Shinkōkai, The Noh Drama (Tokyo and Rutland: Charles E. Tuttle Company, 1955); and René Sieffert, La tradition secrète du Nô (Paris: Gallimard, 1960).

2. Zeami's "treatises" on Nō were discovered only in 1908. The quotations from his work on yūgen are taken from Sources of Japanese Tradition, compiled by Ryusaku Tsunoda, Wm. Theodore de Bary, and Donald Keene (New York: Columbia University Press, 1958), pp. 288-291.

3. Ibid., p. 284.

4. Leonard Cabell Pronko, Theatre East and West (Berkeley and Los Angeles: University of California Press, 1967), p. 86.

5. René Sieffert, La tradition secrète du Nô, p. 53.

6. Japanese Classics Translation Committee, The Noh Drama, pp. ix-x.

7. Makoto Ueda, Literary and Art Theories in Japan (Cleveland: The Press of Western Reserve University, 1967), p. 60.

8. Japanese Classics Translation Committee, The Noh Drama, p. x.

It is, in some ways, unfortunate that the "vocabulary" of traditional Japanese aesthetics is limited to so few basic concepts. The Japanese, in fact, did not so much develop an "aesthetics" in the philosophical sense familiar to us (as a form of theoretical understanding and conceptual analysis), as they elaborated a splendid <u>aesthetic preference</u>. The few aesthetic concepts like <u>aware</u> ("gentle sorrow" appropriate to certain things and events) and <u>sabi</u> ("aesthetic pleasure of the old, the tarnished"), as indeed <u>yūgen</u>, were called upon to cover a wide range of experience and were seldom given any very precise articulation.

9. Raymond Bayer, "The Essence of Rhythm," in Susanne K. Langer, editor, <u>Reflections on Art</u> (Baltimore: The John Hopkins Press, 1959), p. 187.

10. H. Osborne, <u>Theory of Beauty: An Introduction to Aesthetics</u> (New York: Philosophical Library Inc., 1953), p. 77.

Bare Willows and Distant Mountains

Ma Yüan, late 12th century-early 13th century Sung. *Bare Willows and Distant Mountains*, 14. 61. Courtesy of Museum of Fine Arts, Boston, Massachusetts. Chinese and Japanese Special Fund.

The Massacre of the Innocents
Courtesy of Kunsthistorisches Museum, Vienna.

PIETER BRUEGEL AND MA YÜAN: A PHILOSOPHIC INQUIRY INTO THE POSSIBILITIES OF COMPARATIVE CRITICISM

"There is no other artist," writes Otto Benesch, "who could have surpassed Bruegel in this amazing grasp of the soul of Nature. . . . [Pieter] Bruegel [1525/30-1569] in his paintings and drawings has definitely conquered the idea of the universe as an infinite which has form and shape subservient to great cosmic laws."[1]

According to Ching Hao, a Chinese landscape painter of the tenth century, there are four kinds of painters, ranked by descending merit: (1) shên, the "divine" (one who "makes no effort but achieves the forms spontaneously by following the transformations of Nature"); (2) miao, the "wonderful" or "mysterious" (one who "penetrates with his thoughts the nature of everything in heaven and earth, and thus the things flow out of his brush in accordance with the truth of the motif"); (3) ch'i, the "clever" (one who "draws vast outlines, which are not in accordance with the truth of the motif; the things he makes. . . have neither reason nor resemblance"); and (4) ch'iao, the "skillful" (one who "carves out and pieces together scraps of beauty which but seem in accordance with the great principles," being just imitative in nature).[2]

If Ching Hao were to accept Benesch's evaluation of Bruegel, it is clear the Chinese scholar would have placed Bruegel in his second, and not in his first or highest category.

Why is it that someone like Bruegel, who is so highly regarded by a typical modern Western scholar, would be treated by a traditional Chinese scholar, according to his aesthetic standards, as being second class? What are the basic conditions for interpreting and evaluating art-works from other cultures? Can meaningful comparisons be made between works of art from different traditions and cultures? In short: What are the possibilities of comparative criticism?

I

Monroe C. Beardsley has observed that "the possibility of literary criticism presupposes the possibility of keeping artistic judgments _distinct_ from other sorts; but . . . that it does not preclude the possibility that artistic judgments are _connected_ in complicated ways with other sorts."[3] In comparative criticism which seeks understanding from a multicultural standpoint of appreciation these possibilities must be clearly acknowledged.

A special problem for comparative criticism arises, though, from the difficulty that an obserer from one tradition has in getting from the art-work as a "physical object," and the judgments made about it, to the work of art as an "aesthetic object" in another culture because of the object's alienability. We feel uneasy when we confront an unfamiliar work from a tradition different from our own. One feels something of this strangeness with unfamiliar works in one's own tradition, to be sure, but with works from other cultures we feel this strangeness to a qualitatively different degree. The alien work evokes both confusion and fascination; it engenders hostility and yet attraction, but with the dominant feeling being one of puzzlement and repulsion, with these elements attaching themselves for us to the work itself and preventing us thereby from apprehending the work as it has its own being.

One of the peculiarities of comparative criticism is that those dimensions of the art-work which stand most in the way of a full aesthetic experience, and thus also correct judgment, become for the experiencer constitutive of the work that is judged. When one cannot get to the art-work in the fullness of its aesthetic being one tends to take it as just an icon or historical specimen--that is to say, as an "entity" laden with non-aesthetic or extra-aesthetic content. Or, at the other extreme, one takes whatever aesthetic essence one discerns as the work itself.

Normally in aesthetic experience we move from the "physical object" (the art-work as just a physical thing, as it is reducible to physical description) or the "historical artifact" (the art-work as a specimen for historical-cultural analysis, as it is a bearer of extra-aesthetic meaning) to the "aesthetic object" (the art-work *qua* art-work) with its essential aesthetic qualities. With the alien work (e.g., Chinese calligraphy for one who doesn't know Chinese; Indian dance-drama for one who doesn't know the *mūdras*) we often go directly to the essentially aesthetic; that is, we overlook everything but the purely formal qualities of the work. We have the curious situation of our "having an aesthetic experience," but of our not really experiencing the art-work in its own being as an art-work.

The most important problem that we face here, then, is: What kind and quality of knowledge do we need to have of an art-work from another culture and of the culture itself in order that we may get to the art-work in its full--and not just *either* iconographic *or* purely formal--aesthetic potential?

To answer this I think it is necessary that we distinguish four "strata of meaning" or, what would be better called for our purpose, "dimensions of aesthetic relevance," the concrete apprehension of which, in varying degrees with respect to different individual works of art, is necessary for the apprehension and aesthetic appreciation of the art-work.[4] These dimensions do not exhaust the possible kinds of meaning in art; and indeed certain individual works might be deficient in one or more of these dimensions. The dimensions, in other words, are <u>possibilities</u> of aesthetic relevance.

1. <u>Cultural-Authorial Weltanschauung</u>.

In "The Massacre of the Innocents" (Vienna)[5] Bruegel presents us with a scene of human horror; but one whose horror is negated or minimized for us by our having to adopt the viewpoint of nature--a viewpoint which is indifferent to human events. If we were forced by the composition to take a strictly human viewpoint and to be a mere witness to nature's icy indifference, the horror of the scene would only be increased; but we are, on the contrary, compelled to see the massacre from nature's "objectivity" or, which is the same thing, from its indifferent subjectivity. For Bruegel, nature is an ensouled mechanism. Unlike the medieval "dual realism" of a painter like Raphael, who accepts the scholastic universe of two orders of being, each of which is real, with the one deriving its reality through participation in the other,[6] Bruegel's universe, being nonhierarchical, is thoroughly dualistic. Although Bruegel died in 1569, which is nearly thirty years before Descartes' birth (in 1596), we can, I think, speak of his expressing a Cartesian dualism (or, at least, a Newtonian view of the universe). Nature (the <u>res</u> <u>extensa</u>, the extended world) is utterly distinct from Mind (the <u>res</u> <u>cogitans</u>, the world of thought): one does not derive from the other, nor does one participate in the affairs of the other. Nature is essentially mechanical; it goes its way oblivious to human purposes and actions.

To speak of an artist expressing a <u>Weltanschauung,</u> as we have done, does not mean, however, that the artist is expressing some kind of independently thought-out, consistent, philosophical argument or perspective. An artist, like most persons, is not usually aware, in any lucid intellectual sense, of his basic presuppositions. In short, it is not that an artist has a separate philosophical understanding which he then strives to express in his art, rather the artist's vision and his work are created and presented as one. But because an artist is not self-consciously aware of a philosophy does not mean, on the other hand, that underlying attitudes and principles of a philosophical character are absent from his work. On the contrary, they are there at the most comprehensive level of the work's meaning. And to experience the work as it is, as it has its being in its cultural-authorial matrix requires that one have a knowledge and sympathetic understanding of (but not necessarily agreement with) this <u>Weltanschauung</u>.

According to Gustav Glück, "Bruegel describes more than he teaches; he makes a statement without pronouncing judgment; he renders pure reality without criticism but seen with the incomparable eye of an artist."[7] But Glück then goes on to say that "Bruegel's habit of concealing the real subject of a picture and letting it disappear in the surrounding masses may be explained by his opinion of the world, which he considered to be topsy-turvey and wrong-headed, blind to the importance even of the most momentous occurrences."[8] For Bruegel, then, artistic insight calls for the intellectual realization of a single "lawfully regulated totality": it requires the understanding that nature is an infinite, vital domain that is independent of, and sundered from, the mind of man.[9] The insight would not require the realization, through intuitive identification, of a spiritual and rhythmic principle of being, and the attempt to embody that principle spontaneously in art.

For the Chinese painter, of at least one major tradition of Chinese art, such an intuitive identification with nature is essential. The first of the famous six canons of Chinese painting set down by Hsieh Ho in the fifth century is <u>ch'i-yun shêng-tung</u>, translated as "resonance or vibration of the vitalizing spirit and movement of life" (Sirén), or "rhythmic vitality, or spiritual rhythm expressed in the movement of life" (Binyon), or "the harmonizing movement of lifebreath" (Contag).[10] This most important of the canons or principles clearly demands that the artist identify himself with a spiritual vitality (<u>ch'i</u>), a movement of life (<u>shêng-tung</u>) that is pervasive in nature. Spirit is universal: every object in nature embodies it and is enlivened by it. And this power of vitality, this subtle natural-spiritual rhythm, must resound in the painting. The painting must be alive with the very life of nature.

According to the great Taoist master Chüang Tzu, to whom later Chinese artists often referred, "Only the truly intelligent understand the principle of identity. They do not view things as apprehended by themselves subjectively, but transfer themselves into the position of the thing viewed."[11] Bruegel's universe is one that is apprehended "subjectively," which is to say that it is treated as a pure <u>object</u>; for the Sung painter, following Chüang Tzu, there is no real or enduring distinction between subject and object, between man and nature, insofar as they are in perfect rhythmic accord with each other.

In Ma Yüan's (fl. 1190-1225)[12] "Bare Willows and Distant Mountains"--a typical Southern Sung landscape painting[13]--we see mountains, rivers, trees and things made by man, a house, a bridge, in happy relation with one another. The little human figure in the lower right corner of the fan-shaped album leaf is just another element in the composition. One doesn't feel, as with Bruegel's "Massacre," that the unity of the work is achieved by a compositional unification of two otherwise disparate orders; one feels that the unity of the work is achieved through the expression of that unity that is already there in the world.[14] For Bruegel, man and nature are brought together in the painting; for Ma Yüan, man and nature are in unity and have only to be shown together.

Man's relation to nature, as depicted by Ma Yüan, is thus not one of superiority in either direction. No suggestion is made that man has conquered nature or that nature extends an inexorable control over man. <u>Ch'i</u> binds everything together. Between the being of man and the forces of nature there is a dynamic equilibrium. In the West, as pointed out by George Rowley, "The Middle Ages pictured nature as the handiwork of God; the Renaissance and modern periods resorted to the emphatic attribution of human emotions to natural phenomena. In all of these efforts to make nature seem less alien to man, the emphasis was put upon man's experience of nature and not upon nature for itself."[15] For the Chinese painter (philosopher) there was no need to "make nature seem less alien to man" because for him there was no essential estrangement of man from nature or from God. Nature and man were not created <u>ex nihilio</u> by an extra-natural God, rather they find their source and unity in the natural-spiritual way of all things.

But how do we relate differing world-views to aesthetic judgment? To evaluate properly an art-work, Paul Ziff notes, "one must understand it, appreciate it, much of what is said about a work is directly relevant only to an appreciation of it."[16] But most of the time when we encounter a work from another tradition, like "Bare Willows and Distant Mountains," we do not make aesthetic judgments of it, rather we make intellectual and historical judgments about the <u>Weltanschauung</u> and related matters which it exhibits. We judge the <u>class</u> and not the <u>particular</u> work. We are led to see the art-work as only a <u>type</u> of something which is expressive of a particular cultural-authorial world-view and we miss thereby the individual work itself. What this suggests then is that we must understand the cultural-authorial Weltanschauung not so much in order to judge it or to have it be a basis for substituting a class or objects for the particular work, but to enable us to apprehend the art-work as the art-work which exhibits it.

2. Cultural-Authorial Aesthetic Preference.

Closely related to the first strata of meaning or "dimension of aesthetic relevance," yet separate from it, is the fundamental or most general choices of an aesthetic character that are made of the artist in intimate relation to his culture and which go to inform the aesthetic needs and expectations of the experiencer within the culture. The Japanese fondness for "suggestion," "irregularity," "simplicity" and "perishability,"[17] as expressed in countless works by different artists, form a distinctive aesthetic preference, a kind of cultural style the realization of which is often, within this culture, axiomatic for the right experience of an artwork. The aesthetic preference does not follow in any clear logical way from the cultural-authorial Weltanschauung, but it is always compatible with it and is in a large measure derived from it.[18]

Now the aesthetic preference of a culture, and especially of the Chinese, is often formed by--and is in turn exhibited through--the actual materials employed by the artist. Lawrence Sickman goes so far as to maintain that

> The unique character of Chinese painting developed as a result of the materials used and the kind of format evolved in ancient times. Paintings on silk or on paper calls for fluid ink and watercolor pigments, which alone are suitable to those light and absorbent materials.[19]

He then goes on to say that

> Conversely, the distinctive materials and forms were retained over many centuries and developed by artists because these means alone produced the aesthetic qualities which the Chinese most admired.[20]

"Aesthetic preference," as we use it, is a cultural category which, through the artist, informs individual works of art. It is also for the experiencer of the art-work within the culture, a mode of organizing perception. It belongs to the subject as well as to the art-object insofar as it forms the basis of his aesthetic expectations and needs. A cultural-authorial aesthetic preference must, however, be distinguished from "taste." Taste has to do with qualitative discernment within a range of accepted possibilities or "styles." Aesthetic preference is that which establishes the range itself. I might prefer "classical" stability to "romantic" movement, a Poussin rather than a Delacroix, and I might rate David higher than Poussin, but these discernments and preferences are already taking place within a tradition that has established itself on more fundamental preferences--for colors, shapes, perspectives, motifs. Taste is an individual possession; aesthetic preference belongs to a culture and conditions, at the most fundamental level, an individual's taste.

Aesthetic preference applies then both to subject-matter considerations and to aesthetic content as such. "In Bruegel's imagination," writes Glück, "Bible subjects become intensely real; he sees the events of the Bible as scenes of exuberant peasant life. He prefers those aspects of the story that give him the opportunity of painting vast multitudes in continual movement."[21] And "As in the *Procession to Calvary*," F. Grossman notes, "Bruegel has here [in "The Massacre of the Innocents"] represented the biblical scene as a contemporary event, a punitive expedition to a Flemish village, thus endowing it with an extreme intensity and poignancy."[22]

With respect to Chinese art Lawrence Binyon has pointed out that

> . . . the thoughts underlying certain phases of Chinese art will seem peculiarly modern, especially the acceptance of man's true place in the vastness of the universe, the intuition of a continuity of life through all creation, the sympathy with every form of life

outside humanity no less than within it. Hence the absence of what European Art has found the most expressive of all symbols, the nude human form. Hence the discovery of landscape as an independent art centuries before it was anything in Europe but a setting and background for human events; hence the choice of flowers and birds, with us placed in a minor category, as motives equally significant with human figures.[23]

Osvald Sirén relates this preference to the rather low status accorded sculpture in ancient China.

Sculpture was never classified among the fine arts in Old China, a condition which is no doubt closely connected with the fact that the human figure--the main motive of Western sculpture--never was accorded a place of prominence in Chinese art.[24]

The rather limited range of motifs in Chinese painting is often thought to be the result of certain Confucian moral constraints. But the lack, for instance, of "tragic" themes or of the depiction of human-made horrors (of a Chinese Goya) is not because the artist believed that only certain things or events were morally fit to be subjects of artistic representation,[25] it was because personal reaction to the events and the events themselves tend to stand in direct violation of that natural-spiritual rhythm which governs life. It was because human-made horrors were un-natural, according to the profound sense that "natural" had to the Chinese, that they were rejected by the Chinese artist and his culture.[26]

But this much Confucianism is clearly operative: moral standing and achievement means nothing if not self-restraint and "cultivation." And as Roger Fry notes:

> A Michelangelo is unthinkable in the atmosphere of Chinese art; still more perhaps an El Greco letting himself go whithersoever the exaltation of his fevered imagination carried him. This kind of exaltation, as well as dramatic intensity of human feeling, seem unknown.[27]

What this simply means, though, for comparative criticism is that knowing the cultural-authorial aesthetic preference (and, if appropriate, recognizing it as an alternative aesthetically valid possibility) facilitates--and is necessary for--the recognition of the quality of the alien art-work. One cannot get to the art-work properly as an aesthetic object unless one is able to allow the aesthetic preference to become a mode of organizing one's own perception. The preference for the exaggerated, the symbolic, the larger than life expression to be found in so much of Indian art; the preference for the restrained, subtle and yet elegant expression to be found in Chinese art, with to be sure an enormous range allowed for individual expression;[28] as indeed the more robust humanism and play of forms and colors of a Western painter, must be discerned, with the individual works of art being evaluated and interpreted in part by their relation to that aesthetic preference. It would indeed be ludicrous for one to apply mechanically one's "taste" to works from another culture which may have a different aesthetic preference.

3. Formal Content.

By "formal content" I mean the realized composition or design, the resolution of contrasts and tensions, the inner vitality that is the art-work in formal terms. The "formal content" is the primary material, the basic carrier of value, of aesthetic experience.

Roger Fry writes:

> The first thing, I think, that strikes one is the immense part played in Chinese art by linear rhythm. The contour is always the most important feature of the form.
>
> Next we note that that rhythm is almost always of a flowing, continuous character. . . . A painting was always conceived as the visible record of a rhythmic gesture. It was the graph of a dance executed by the hand.[29]

Chinese painting and calligraphy, it is often noted, are closely connected--and, in some ways, impossible to separate.[30] The formal content in much of Chinese (especially landscape) art is immediately evident and given in the brushwork. The rhythmic flow and subtle tonal gradations, the suggestive line rather than bold statement or minutely detailed representation, the careful structuring of space, so effortlessly achieved, it seems to us, by the simple means of brush and ink, constitutes the formal dimension of the work. "Gifted with a fastidious taste for harmony in color," writes Binyon, "the Chinese are reticent in its use. No art again is more skilled in bringing out the value of space, of the empty intervals, in a design."[31]

George Rowley has noted that

> The Chinese perfected the principle of the three depths, according to which spatial depth was marked by a foreground, middle distance, and far distance, each parallel to the picture plane, so that the eye leapt from one distance to the next through a void of space.[32]

This leaping of the eye, it was expected, brings the viewer out of the narrow confines of a fixed self-centered perspective into the subtle and infinite space of Nature. The "voids" are not empty, they are full--and the viewer was to be free to have his being echoed in them.

Man's being-in-nature is realized by Ma Yüan by the flexible control which the formal content of his work exercises over the viewer. Lawrence Sickman describes the general practice of Sung painters clearly in these words:

> There is no final vanishing point, or one-point perspective. Each element is presented in the most typical or pictorially satisfying aspect. The observer may be looking down upon the scene from a great elevation. . .or he may, in imagination, stand in the foreground and look up at the towering heights above.[33]

The control is thus one which opens up a wide range of visual possibilities. The observer is not given a fixed place of reference rather he moves, as it were, in and through the landscape as though he were walking there.

The formal content of Chinese art is what it is in its rhythmic vitality and spiritual resonance by virtue of both the world-view/aesthetic-preference complex and the materials used to establish it--and the method of creativity appropriate to them. Both the theoretical view-preference and the materials of the art make for a highly disciplined and (perhaps paradoxically, tradition-bound) spontaneity in creativity. "He who deliberates and moves the brush intent upon making a picture misses . . . the art of painting."[34] Spontaneity for the Sung painter does not of course mean some kind of uninhibited "action painting;" rather it means the natural and highly disciplined expression of the unity of being that is achieved by direct aesthetic awareness. This unity is not an abstraction, a concept, but a vital spiritual life which enlivens the artist and informs his work. A Wang Wei can thus write:

> The wind rises from the green forest, and foaming water rushes in the stream. Alas! Such paintings cannot be achieved by the physical movements of the fingers and the hand, but only by the spirit entering into them. This is the nature of painting.[35]

Mastery of the brushwork which exhibits this spontaneity means complete control of the uninterrupted flow of ink. "The individual character of the painter's brushwork, which is the expression of his qualities as a man," writes Sickman, "must be unfaltering and sustained. No second thoughts, corrections, or smudging-over are possible."[36]

Deliberation means calculation; the self-conscious intellectual arrangement of elements or structural features. The thinking mind, by its deliberations, becomes evident in the painting. There is a greater articulation and precision, a greater awareness of individual objects in their strict givenness, in Bruegel than in Ma Yüan. In Bruegel we have a whole constituted by its parts; in Ma Yüan we have a whole that controls and determines its parts. One could trace the geometry, as it were, in Bruegel's "Massacre;" one can only sense the movements within the whole in Ma Yüan's "Willows."

The spontaneity that is exhibited formally in the art-work is, as indicated, bound very closely to tradition and to a discipline which requires mastery over innumerable "canons" established by previous masters of the art. Chinese art has for ages been an art for the connoisseur. The sophisticated connoisseurship that developed in China allowed the artist to function for the most part within well-defined criteria of excellence. We in the West tend to look upon this rather heavy tradition-bound set of standards as a burden that the artist had to tolerate (or a hardship that he had to react against). With few (but notable) exceptions, however, the Chinese artist saw the presence of this highly refined and sharpened taste of his potential critic as an opportunity and challenge. It enabled him to work according to, in obedience to, recognized and clearly understood standards and it thus enabled him to exercise his powers--and even originality--to the fullest. He did not have to waste his time and effort in doing something "new" for its own sake; rather he could devote himself entirely to the task of bringing his own feelings and intuitions to articulation within the structures of a demanding taste.

Wen C. Fong has written:

> Chinese painting, being closely related to Chinese calligraphy, was based on fixed graphic form-types and compositional schemes. Wu Li (1632-1718) wrote: 'To paint without Sung and Yüan styles as a foundation is like playing chess without chess pieces. Facing the empty chess board where does one begin?' When a game or sport is played with set forms and rules, the emphasis is on individual action and performance. In Chinese painting, as in calligraphy, each form is built up of a familiar set of brushstrokes, but the execution of these form-types is, each time, a new and unique act.[37]

Now the continuity of formal-content presentations in Chinese art can, of course, be over-emphasized; but even when so-called radical breaks in various periods take place there is a harking back to the "ancients" for stimulation and instruction.

Max Loehr describes the contrast between the Sung and Yüan periods in these terms:

> The Yüan situation was without precedent in so far as style, no longer given by tradition, became the fundamental artistic problem. Each of the great Yüan masters created his own style. Accordingly, there was no stylistic unity in that period, although we may discover certain tendencies common to all of the

> masters; they all rejected the ideas of Sung;
> they all tended toward the suppression of
> tone and wash, except Wu Chen; and they all
> seemed concerned with structural principles
> and a new linearity.[38]

He goes on to say with reference to the Ming period:

> Ancient styles, to be sure, were always
> studied, however not as motifs or pictorial
> content but as means. This was true also
> of the Yüan masters. Now, in the Ming period,
> the ancient styles up to late Sung, irrevocably
> final and beyond dispute, acquire an aura
> of truth. They are now approached, in a
> spirit of scholasticism, as Reality.[39]

The clinging to tradition in Chinese painting seems to suggest that the Chinese--as at times classical-minded artists and critics in the West--believed that there are certain universal and enduring principles of aesthetic validity. A crucial problem that must be faced in dealing with "formal content" (and which may perhaps be given its clearest formulation in the context of comparative criticism) is: <u>Are formal principles in art entirely culture-bound or are there universal principles of aesthetic rightness</u>?

It is often asked: Are there "structural markers" in music that are rooted in our organic being so that by determining patterns of expectation, tension, fulfillment and release they serve as universal conditions for aesthetically pleasing musical

form? Are there proportions in architecture the
presence of which in buildings are universally per-
ceivable as aesthetically right?--and so on. These
questions are to a considerable extent strictly empirical, with affirmative answers not easy to come
by.[40] The questions, however, in any event, are not,
it seems to me, the best way to raise the issue
either for aesthetics in general or for comparative
criticism in particular; for whether or not there
are general principles (or laws) which may be said
to govern formal contents there are assuredly no spe-
cifiable qualities which <u>taken by themselves</u> will
make the art-work attractive or "beautiful."
This is so because it is never the case that any
single quality or factor is sufficient for aesthetic rightness and validity. The mere presence of a
pleasing color harmony or "proper" musical sequence,
taken in isolation, hardly insures, when present in
an art-work, anything of compelling aesthetic interest. Indeed a proportion or color scheme that is
quite "correct" in itself could be entirely inappro-
priate--in say an expressionistic painting. And a
distorted proportion or a disharmonious color arrangement, on the other hand, which if taken by themselves would not be aesthetically pleasing, may
nevertheless function rightly in a given work and
contribute significantly to its validity.

The "formal content" of a work of art is there in the work integrally--and must be discerned not as pieces which may embody principles but as a gestalt, as a structured or organic whole. The formal content of an art-work, what this comes down to mean, is always unique. It is the particular art-work as particular, as absolutely irreplaceable, in its own vital being of line and color, pattern, harmony, contrast, tension which is the formal content of aesthetic experience--East and West.

One further problem that arises in this context has to do with our experiencing an object in satisfying aesthetic terms (via formal content) as a work of art when it was not intended to be a work of art (as we are prone to understand the term) in the culture in which it was produced. A Paleolithic cave painting as well as many medieval Indian statues were not, it is widely believed, created for the sake of aesthetic contemplation but as they were instruments either for magical rite or religious worship. According to the intention of their makers these objects, so many believe, should be taken as historical artifacts and not as works of art. Objects of this sort, however, while not intended as objects created by a self-conscious will as expressive forms that are satisfyingly contemplated, were intended no doubt to be aesthetically pleasing in formal terms, and if they can in addition easily bear the weight of iconological analysis, then I see no reason why they shouldn't qualify as "works of art." Because an object was intended to be used for various essentially non-aesthetic purposes does not make it less interesting for us if indeed it is able to stand up, as it were, under formal, iconographic and iconological analysis.

The distinction, then, between an art-work and an icon or artifact must, I think, be drawn not in terms of how an artist or culture intended the use of the object but in terms of the manner in which aesthetic meaning is established by the work. The icon or artifact draws its meaning entirely (or, at least, predominately) in terms of its <u>subject-matter</u> (or "representational symbolism") while the art-work does so in terms of its <u>content</u>. With the icon, or with inferior works of art, meaning is essentially external to the work itself; it is conventional, historical, just symbolic in the literal sense of "standing for" something else. Meaning derived from subject-matter, what the work is <u>about</u>, is always translatable into non-aesthetic terms. The meaning was established prior to and it remains independent of the object which exhibits it.[41]

With the art-work, on the other hand, meaning is essentially internal to the work. It is there uniquely in the work; it is, as content, what the work itself is. The meaning of an art-work has no existence apart from the concrete particular work. The meaning, in short, is <u>presentative</u> rather than just <u>representative</u>.

4. <u>Symbolic Values</u>.

"Symbol," we are told, "in its original context, meant secret sign of recognition." It "stems from the Greek <u>symballo</u>, to throw together, join, or unite."[42] Symbols or, I would prefer, "symbolic values" are widely recognized to be the most basic carrier of meaning in art.

Now many schemes of symbolism in art have been developed, but in order to identify some problem areas in comparative criticism we may draw upon Philip Wheelwright's ordering of what he calls "tensive symbols"[43] and classify symbolic values in art very broadly and rather crudely (and without any pretense that the classification is complete or exhaustive) into three main divisions, the first and second of which have several sub-types. These are:

(1) <u>natural symbolic values</u>: When the "sun" is used to symbolize "heat," when "bright light" is used for "spiritual illumination" we have examples of natural symbolic values. They are of two kinds: (a) the <u>empirical</u> and (b) the <u>archetypal</u>. "Sun" standing for "heat" derives from the observation of

a certain regularity in nature; the relation is learned directly in experience; the symbol has a highly restricted range of signification when used in this context. "Bright light" standing for "spiritual illumination," on the other hand, as pointed out by Wheelright,[44] tends toward the archetypal; it derives from unconscious associations, the relation seemingly being a given of experience; it has a wider connotative efficacy and hence a wider range of signification than the "empirical."

Natural symbolic values obviously impose no special problem for comparative criticism as they do not stand in any special way as a barrier to cross-cultural interpretation and evaluation. They are, in fact, the most readily understood symbolic values precisely because of their presumed universality. They are also the least interesting aesthetically (probably because of that presumed universality), being transparent in content.[45]

(2) <u>conventional symbolic values</u>: A conventional symbol is not derived from any natural or apparently necessary relation between it and what is symbolized but is essentially arbitrary; it is learned through education.

There are many grades that may be distinguished in this category, from those which border on the natural ("cow" for "fertility") to those that appear to be purely cultural ("dove" for "peace"), but for our purpose we may distinguish here roughly between (a) <u>environmental</u>, (b) <u>cultural</u> and (c) <u>personal</u> symbolic values. The environmental rests upon the suggestiveness of the object itself ("willow tree" for "sadness") while the cultural depends upon specific cultural beliefs or religio-historical events ("cross" for "suffering"), and the personal upon the particular subjective choice of an artist (Rilke's "angel").

The environmental and cultural symbolic values are shared unconsciously, as it were, by the members of a culture and they enjoy rather wide ranges and levels of meaning. The personal symbolic values on the other hand, while still being conventional in character, are essentially constructs of the artistic imagination and function as carriers of a personal vision. They work properly as symbols only in the context of the art-work itself; their value as symbol, in other words, is locked into the work. Yeat's "dolphin," Kafka's "castle," to take further examples from literary art, have their power in their revelation of existential meanings and relationships as given in the works in which they appear.

Now it is often thought that the conventional symbolic values, more than anything else, set up barriers between the art-work of X culture and the observer from Y culture, for in many cases where these values are employed extensively they depend for their efficacy upon culture-bound experiences and associations; their full experience is therefore available only to one for whom these experiences and associations are, as it were, second nature. Conventional symbolic values, and especially with the class of cultural symbols, convey a special meaning; they do not so much disclose or uncover new meaning as they transmit old meaning; they are, in other words, thoroughly historical in character.

The symbolic values of an art-work, moreover, are not something that is superadded to its formal content in some arithmetic way, rather they are what the lines, colors, shapes are in their own being as meaning-ful. This means that to experience the art-work as it has its own authentic being one must (always to a greater or less degree) assimilate its symbolic values directly as contents of a comprehensive aesthetic experience.

This dimension of aesthetic relevance reveals, then, that most of the time most of us do indeed miss a good deal of what is there in our experience of works from other cultures. But this is not to suggest that the alien work is just to remain for us as something strange and inscrutable, rather it is to suggest that one simply must learn enough about the conventional symbols from another culture to have a generally correct idea of what is going on in a given work (which often means no more than not having an erroneous idea); but--and this is a crucial point-- unless the aesthetic quality rests entirely upon the associations themselves (in which case one might reasonably suspect that there is something lacking in the work, it being overly didactic) this learning should in most cases be sufficient to take one a long way.[46] In fact, in terms of the possibilities of aesthetic judgment, the outsider might actually have something of an advantage, for it is often the case that one knows too much in experiencing a work from one's own culture--the conventional symbols have so rich an association-complex for one that it is difficult to get beyond the literal or representational meaning to what is being said aesthetically. As a carryover from our ordinary perception we tend often to rest content once we have recognized certain conventional symbolic values and we thus fail to move deeper in our experience of the work that embodies them.[47]

One further problem, though, that does arise here is that of understanding the art-work (via conventional symbolic values) as the work is part of the art history of its culture insofar as the art-work might be understandable only as it is within that history. Richard Wollheim has pointed out that

> In 1917 Marcel Duchamp submitted to an art exhibition a porcelain urinal with the signature of the manufacturer attached in his, Duchamp's, handwriting. The significance of such iconoclastic gestures is manifold; but insofar as the gesture is to be seen as falling within art, it has been argued (by Adrian Stokes) that this requires that we project on to the object's 'patterns and shapes . . . a significance learned from many pictures and sculptures.' In other words, it would be difficult to appreciate what Duchamp was trying to do without an overall knowledge of the history of art's metamorphoses.[48]

This problem is especially acute in much of later Chinese painting where, in several instances, the work of art is really just a commentary on other works of art.[49] But in terms of the possibilities of interpretation and evaluation the difficulty is partly mitigated by the fact that once again the more the requirement for "a knowledge of the history of art's metamorphoses" is needed for an appreciation of the aesthetic value of a work, the less likely it is that the work will have that value as an intrinsic character.

(3) <u>essential symbolic values</u>: The last form, level or kind of symbolism in art that we need to distinguish is fundamentally different from the other

types (and perhaps shouldn't really be listed as one of them; but the paucity of our classificatory methods and means compels us to place it here anyway), for this type pertains strictly to the work of art *qua* work of art. In other words, this type of symbolism is not so much in the work as it is the work itself as it participates in--and as it has own presentative reality in--spiritual being. Through its formal content and other dimensions of aesthetic relevance, the art-work--if it is a good work--is perceived here in its fullest qualitative efficacy as a unique concentration of meaning and value. The essential symbolic level is achieved when the artwork as such uncovers and reveals spiritual being in its own aesthetic being. The art-work as essential symbol is its meaning, its own form as a radiant form. And here there are no cross-cultural barriers, for when one attains recognition of this level of the work, in and through the other dimensions, one is involved not with a cultural perspective on reality but with insight into basic human being and the world. Interpretation and evaluation here involve the capacity of the art-work to bring the experiencer of it to that heightened, intense awareness which the art-work itself makes manifest.

III

We have distinguished four dimensions of aesthetic relevance for comparative criticism with the aim of providing an answer to the basic question: What kind and quality of knowledge do we need to have of an art-work from another culture and of the culture itself in order that we may get to the art-work in its full aesthetic potential? The recognition and sympathetic understanding of the cultural-authorial Weltanschauung that informs an individual work of art was seen as crucial, although it must be admitted that for many persons such a recognition and understanding is exceedingly difficult to achieve. Centered so deeply as most of us are in our own tidy (or sloppy, as the case may be) world-view we find ourselves at a loss to begin even to understand the essential ideas of other cultures. But as the fault lies with us and not with the ideas themselves, it is correctable.

The cultural-authorial aesthetic preference of a culture is always closely related to the Weltanschauung. It governs choices both of subject-matter or motif and the most fundamental aesthetic values that are at play in the culture and are accordingly operative in the individual art-work. The particular materials of the art which are employed in the culture, e.g., the strict economy of ink and brush in much of Chinese art, are of great significance, with some understanding of the possibilities and limitations of these means being important. The aesthetic preference, however, is something that can be assimilated as an organizing mode of perception and, when so assimilated, may contribute to our apprehension of the aesthetic quality of the individual work of art.

The formal content is the work of art in formal terms and is obviously the primary stuff of the aesthetic experience of the work. It is what it is in terms of the artist's manner of creativity, and it is available to aesthetic sensitivity wherever found. Without having to appeal to any presumed universal or absolute principles of art we can still identify a universal potentiality for recognizing aesthetic excellence in works of art.

A work of art, though, at least traditionally, is not just a combination of abstract ideas and formal content; rather it embodies a range of meaning that is wedded directly, in a variety of ways, to formal content. In short, there are various kinds of symbolic values which have to be recognized and understood. Some of these, like the natural symbolic values, do not pose any special problems for comparative criticism; others, like various conventional cultural symbols do impose difficulties, for an outsider can never experience certain symbols with the same range of associations and memories that the insider does. But a certain basic understanding can take the outsider a long way and he might even enjoy a peculiar advantage over the insider in not getting so entangled in conventional meanings that he misses the individual art-work itself.

An art-work is a multi-dimensional, as well as many leveled, object--for it is at once an historical-cultural thing (open to socio-cultural analysis as a transparent object for understanding a civilization) and an aesthetic object. But this does not mean that the critic or philosophical viewer as such must be an art historian, sociologist, linguist or whatever in order to interpret and evaluate works of art from other cultures, for this would mean separating out the meaning from the aesthetic content, and one is not then dealing with the art-work as an art-work but as something else. In the final analysis the strictly cultural factors are to be recognized, discerned, comprehended for the sake of realizing the aesthetic content of the work. This then is the possibility of comparative criticism; it may enable us to apprehend the art-work in its full cultural and individual authenticity as the particular work that it is.

Comparative criticism does not mean making cross-cultural judgments of the sort 'X work of Western art (say a Mozart concerto) is better or worse

74

that Y work of Eastern art (say an Indian rāga)'. This type of judgment presupposes the possibility of formulating a standard of aesthetic judgment that is not itself culture-conditional or culture-bound, a possibility the realization of which is difficult if not impossible to conceive.

The task of comparative criticism is just to pave the way, as it were, for one to get to the essential aesthetic being of the art-work in the fullness of the art-work's own being.

Notes

1. Otto Benesch, *The Art of the Renaissance in Northern Europe* (Cambridge: Harvard University Press, 1945), p. 104.

2. This classification is set forth in a famous essay by Ching Hao called *Pi Fa Chi* ("Records of Brush Work"). Ching's classification is a modification of earlier ones by Chu Ching-hsüan in *T'ang Ch'ao Ming Hua Lu*, written at the end of the T'ang dynasty, and by Huang Hsiu-fu in *I Chou Ming Hua Lu*, published in 1005. These earlier versions were themselves based on Chang Huai-küan's classification of calligraphic writings in *Shu Tuan*, written 724-77. Chang Huai-küan distinguished three classes of painters; the divine (*shên*), the wonderful (*miao*) and the skillful (*nêng*). Chu Ching-hsüan added a fourth category *i*, the spontaneous or impetuous, but it is not clear where it belongs in the hierarchy as Chu acknowledges that it may be characterized either as excellent or low. Huang Hsiu-fu, on the other hand, places *i* as the first of the classes and Ching Hao replaces it with the category of the "clever." Osvald Sirén notes that "this modification of the scheme proposed by Chu Ching-hsüan and Huang Hsiu-fu may indeed be said to have good reason, because the spontaneously impetuous painters are more difficult to distinguish from the divine than are the clever from the skilful." *The Chinese on the Art of Painting* (New York: Schocken Books, 1963), pp. 41-42. See ibid. appendix IV and also Ching Hao, "Note on Brushwork," trans. by S. Sakanishi, *The Spirit of the Brush* (London: John Murray, 1939), p. 89; and Lawrence Sickman and Alexander Soper, *The Art and Architecture of China* (Balti-

more: Penguin Books, Inc., 1956), p. 104.

3. Monroe C. Beardsley, *The Possibility of Criticism* (Detroit: Wayne State University Press, 1970), p. 90.

4. In his *Studies in Iconology* published in 1939 Erwin Panofsky distinguishes three "strata of meaning" to be found in a work of art. The "strata" are highly suggestive and will be implicitly accounted for in our articulation of dimensions of aesthetic relevance. They are: (1) "Primary or natural subject matter. ... It is apprehended by identifying pure *forms*, that is: certain configurations of line and color. . . as representations of natural *objects* such as human beings, animals... tools and so forth; by identifying their mutual relations as *events*; and by perceiving such *expressional* qualities as the mournful character of a pose or gesture. ... (2) Secondary or conventional subject matter. It is apprehended by realizing ... that a group of figures seated at a dinner table in a certain arrangement and in certain poses represents the Last Supper. ... The identification of such *images*, *stories* and *allegories* is the domain of iconography in the narrower sense of the word. (3) Intrinsic meaning or content. It is apprehended by ascertaining those underlying principles which reveal the basic attitudes of a nation, a period, a class, a religious or philosophical persuasion--unconsciously qualified by one personality and condensed into one work." *Studies in Iconology: Humanistic Themes in the Art of the Renaissance* (Oxford: Oxford University Press, 1939); reprinted in paperback by Harper & Row, 1962. Quotations are taken from the paperback edition, pp. 5-8.

For some applications and criticisms of this

analysis see, Joseph Margolis, "Describing and Interpreting Works of Art," in *Contemporary Studies in Aesthetics*, edited by Francis J. Coleman (New York: McGraw-Hill Book Company, 1968), pp. 187-88; and David Mannings, "Panofsky and the Interpretation of Pictures," *The British Journal of Aesthetics*, Vol. 13, no. 2 (Spring 1973).

    5. Although "The Massacre of the Innocents" is thought by many authorities to be of less artistic value than other of Bruegel's works (see Charles Tolnay, *Pieter Bruegel L'ancien* [Brussells: Nouvelle Société d'Editions, 1935] and Max J. Friedlander, *Die Altniederlandische Malerei*, Vol. XIV, *Pieter Bruegel*, 1937), and it has even been maintained by F. Grossmann that "X-ray photographs ... reveal definitely that Bruegel can have had no great share in the execution [of the Vienna version]" (*The Paintings of Bruegel* [London: Phaidon Press, 1966], p. 199), we have selected it for our comparative analysis because of the sharp contrast in motif and composition it affords with the example from Ma Yüan that we will use. We would also agree with Robert L. Delevoy that "the line-work may seem stiff but there is nothing hesitant about it, and only Bruegel could have supplied the brilliant color orchestration. We find saturated tones, vermillions, yellows, greens and white, and color harmonies that assuredly derive from the palette of the master. ..." *Bruegel*, trans. by Stuart Gilbert (Skira, 1959).

    6. See, for example, his "L'Incoronazine della Vergine," 1503 in the Vatican Gallery. The painting has been described accurately thus: "The 'Coronation' is divided into two distinct portions. Below are the apostles, crowded about the empty sarcophagus of the Virgin, from which spring roses

and lilies; Christ alone, seated in the clouds, places a celestial crown upon the bowed head of his Mother, while a choir of angels plays and sings to them. The upward glances of several of the apostles serve to unite the two portions of the composition." Frank Ray Fraprie, <u>The Raphael Book</u> (Boston: L. C. Page & Co., 1912), p. 39.

    7. Gustav Glück, <u>Pieter Bruegel the Elder</u>, trans. by Eveline Byam Shaw (Paris: The Hyperion Press, 1936), p. 13.

    8. Ibid., p. 14.

    9. Delevoy relates this nicely to the concern at the time with mathematics. "Mathematical perspective," he writes, at once provided the artist with a countercheck on his imagination and, in furthering a cosmic sense of space, inaugurated a new relationship with the outside world giving rise to a whole philosophy of nature. ... This method of research culminated in an image corresponding to the world-picture formulated by the natural philosopher, the concept of an infinitely extended, eternal universe, inseparable from its Maker. ... It fell to Bruegel to implement this new and ampler measure of the universe in his art. <u>Bruegel</u>, p. 29.

    10. William Acker believes this first canon (or Element, as he calls it) to consist in just <u>ch'i-yun</u>, "spirit resonance," with the <u>shêng-tung</u> being an "explanatory equivalent." He sums up his analysis by saying that "I think we may conclude, then, that <u>ch'i yun</u> means that the painter should know how to become filled with <u>ch'i</u> before starting his work, and while painting should remain vibrant with energy or intensely alive, so that what he creates will show evidence of this power and vitality." William R. B. Acker, <u>Some T'ang and Pre-</u>

T'ang Texts on Chinese Painting (Leiden: E. J. Brill, 1954), p. xxxiii. For a criticism of this reading of the Canons see James F. Cahill, "The Six Laws and How to Read Them," Ars Orientalis, IV, 1961, pp. 372-381 and Wen Fong, "On Hsieh Ho's 'Liu-Fa'," Oriental Art, IX, no. 4 (Winter 1963).

11. Chüang Tzu, as quoted in Osvald Sirén, op. cit., p. 24.

12. See Osvald Sirén, Chinese Painting: Leading Masters and Principles (New York: The Ronald Press, 1956), Vol. II, pp. 112 ff. for a biographical sketch of Ma Yüan and his place in Chinese landscape painting.

13. For purposes of our philosophic inquiry into the possibilities of comparative criticism we have selected this work by Ma Yüan as it brings out the underlying philosophic attitudes of the Chinese landscape painter of the time so clearly in its pictorial content and manner and execution, and because works of the Ma-Hsih school are already most familiar to the Westerner. Were this paper intended as a contribution to either Art History or Sinology we would have been extremely wary in selecting a work which could but fortify certain Western stereotypes about what the vast richness of Chinese art consists in. With all due respects to the sentiments of R. H. van Gulik--("It is the study of the artist's technical means that provides a direct and certain approach, whereas abstruse speculation, if divorced from practical knowledge, take one along a circuitous road - and one that moreover as often as not will lead the traveler completely astray" -- Chinese Pictorial Art As Viewed by the Connoisseur [Rome: Instituto Italiano per il Medio ed Estremo Oriente, 1958], p. 368)--it is hoped that the philosophical traveler may be pardoned his

non-connoisseur use of Ma Yüan, and that indeed the connoisseur will sympathize with the philosopher's need for concrete examples in aesthetics.

14. Sirén describes the work in this way: "There is a mountain range rising through light mist in the background, and at its foot a village which is almost hidden. The calm river which is winding down to the lower edge is spanned by a bamboo bridge, and on the spit of low ground that juts out into the river two bare willows sway their plumming branches like quivering tendrils. The atmosphere is suggested by subtle gradations of tone. There is a breath of morning wind touching the tops of the willows. The mist is slowly dissolving--otherwise no movement, no sound, Spring is still hesitating." Chinese Painting, p. 116.

15. George Rowley, Principles of Chinese Painting (Princeton: Princeton University Press, 1959), p. 21.

16. Paul Ziff, "Reasons in Art Criticism," in Art and Philosophy, edited by W. E. Kennick (New York: St. Martin's Press, 1964), p. 607.

17. See Donald Keene, "Japanese Aesthetics," Philosophy East and West, XIX, 3 (July 1969), pp. 293-306.

18. For example, as Michael Sullivan writes: "The very concept of completion is utterly alien to the Chinese way of thinking. The Chinese painter deliberately avoids a complete statement because he knows that we can never know everything, that what we can describe, or 'complete', cannot be true in the larger sense. All he can do is to liberate the imagination and set it wandering over the limitless space of the universe. His landscape is not a final statement, but a starting point; not an end, but the opening of a door." A Short History of Chinese Art

(Berkeley: University of California Press, 1967), p. 183.

19. Lawrence Sickman, Chinese Calligraphy and Painting In the Collection of John M. Crawford, Jr. (New York: The Pierpont Morgan Library, 1962), p. 17.

20. Ibid.

21. Gustav Glück, Pieter Brueghel The Elder, p. 8.

22. F. Grossman, The Paintings of Bruegel (London: Phaidon Press, 1966), p. 199.

23. Lawrence Binyon, Chinese Art (London: Kegan Paul, Trench, Trubner & Co., Ltd., 1935), p. x.

24. Osvald Sirén, in Chinese Art: An Introductory Review of Painting, Ceramics, Textiles, Bronzes, Sculpture, Jade, Etc., edited by Roger Fry, Lawrence Binyon, et al. Burlington Magazine Monograph (London: Bote Batsford Ltd., 1925), p. 47.

25. Although Confucian ethical doctrine seems to have encouraged at times an elevated subject-matter view of painting among critics, this was often a mere paying of lip service to traditional moralistic concerns. See James F. Cahill, "Confucian Elements in the Theory of Painting," in The Confucian Persuasion, edited by Arthur F. Wright (Stanford: Stanford University Press, 1960), p. 121.

26. This is further substantiated by the value that was placed on landscape painting in particular to bring the viewer to feel that he was present in the place represented. "Until the second half of the eleventh century," writes Cahill, "...the notion that a painting of a given object or scene should evoke in the person who sees it thoughts and feelings akin to those that the actual object or scene would evoke, was never seriously challenged." Chinese Painting (Skira, 1960), p. 89.

27. Roger Fry, in Chinese Art: An Introductory Review, p. 4.

28. Contrary to the stereotype belief about the utter impersonality of the Chinese artist, it is clearly evident that much attention was paid to the aesthetic qualities and preferences of individual artists. In fact the earliest Chinese writings on art emphasize more the artistic powers (and moral qualities) of individual artists than they do the aesthetic quality of particular works of art. The artists and not their works as such were ranked according to their merit. This attitude is also (over-) developed later by the wen-jen or "literati" painters (who were all amateurs) to the point where they held that the quality of the painting is always a direct reflection of the personal or human quality of the painter.

29. Roger Fry, in Chinese Art: An Introductory Review, p. 2.

30. Cf. Lawrence Sickman, Chinese Calligraphy and Painting in the Collection of John M. Crawford, Jr., p. 19. "Chinese calligraphy. . . requires mastery over virtually all the same strokes that are used in painting...." William Acker also notes that "the essential criteria by which competent Chinese critics have been accustomed to judge paintings have been mainly the same since the fifth century, when Hsieh Ho wrote the Ku Hua P'in Lu, and that these criteria have been from the very beginning strongly influenced by those obtaining in the art of calligraphy." Some T'ang and Pre-T'ang Texts in Chinese Painting, p. lii.

31. Lawrence Binyon, Chinese Art, p. 7. James Cahill also notes that "In orthodox Chinese styles the color washes are flat and ungraduated; color is almost never used as it is in the West, to model form

or to describe the fall of light on a surface." Chinese Painting, p. 15.

32. George Rowley, Principles of Chinese Painting, p. 64.

33. Lawrence Sickman and Alexander Soper, The Art and Architecture of China, p. 105. See also Benjamin March, "Linear Perspective in Chinese Painting," Eastern Art, edited by Langdon Warner and Horace H. F. Jayne, Vol. III, 1931. March sums up his study in these terms: "...Chinese perspective is characterized in contrast with the Renaissance perspective of the West, by two distinctly typical features--a station-point movable without restriction, or numerous station-points within a single picture; and the drawing of parallel lines as true, rather than apparent, parallels " (p. 139).

34. From Chang Yen-yüan (9th century), Li-tai Ming-hua Chi (Record of Famous Painters of Successive Dynasties) in Sirén, The Chinese on the Art of Painting, p. 24.

35. From ibid., in Sources of Chinese Tradition, edited by Wm. Theodore de Bary, et al. (New York: Columbia University Press, 1960), p. 295.

36. Lawrence Sickman, Chinese Calligraphy and Painting In the Collection of John M. Crawford, Jr., p. 19.

37. Wen C. Fong, "Orthodoxy and Change in Early Ch'ing Landscape Painting," Oriental Art, XVI, no. 1, p. 38. Victoria Contag elaborates on this point in these words: "In China a picture painted in such and such a way by a great master is later imitated in the identical form, even by great artists....What the Chinese connoisseur values in an imitative work of this kind is the new personal handwriting. Connoisseurs can recognize a well-known master by the brushwork of a small detail of rock as clearly as we

can see from the address on a letter which friend or relative has written it." Chinese Masters of the 17th Century, trans. by Michael Bullock (London: Lund Humphries, 1969), p. 3.

38. Max Loehr, "Chinese Painting After Sung," Yale Art Gallery, Ryerson Lecture, March 2, 1967.

39. Ibid.

40. There has not, to my knowledge, been many experiments carried out in this area with a high degree of scientific sophistication. Some basic work in "comparative perception" of the sort done by Profs. Segall, Cambell and Hersovits (See Science, 139 [1963], p. 769), however, suggests that even very rudimentary perceptual acts are often culture-bound to a considerable degree.

41. Another example of this might be the many collosal Buddhas to be found (e.g., at Bamiyan in Afghanistan) where the expressive affect is achieved not through any intrinsic aesthetic quality so much as by means of the psychological associations with sheer-size--suggesting and evoking awe.

42. Peter Fingesten, "The Six-Fold Law of Symbolism," The Journal of Aesthetics and Art Criticism, XXI, 4 (Summer 1963), p. 387.

43. See his Metaphor and Reality (Bloomington: Indiana University Press, 1962), chapter V. Wheelwright distinguishes between "steno-symbols" like those in logic which have "a public exactitude, an uncompromising identity of reference for all who use them correctly" and "tensive symbols" which "cannot be entirely stipulative, inasmuch as its essential tension draws life from a multitude of associations, subtly and for the most part subconsciously interrelated." He goes on to distinguish five types of tensive symbols in terms of their "grades of comprehension or breath of appeal": (1) presiding

image of a single poem [or work of art in general]--a symbol which has not had any ancestry and is influential only in the art-work (Mallarmé's "faun"); (2) personal symbol--a symbol with a uniquely woven pattern of associations (Crane's "Atlantis"); (3) symbols of ancestral vitality--symbols lifted by the artist from earlier artistic sources (Eliot's "harlot" in The Waste Land); (4) symbols of cultural range--"Those which have a significant life for members of a community, of a cult, or of a larger secular or religious body;" and (5) arche-typal symbols--"symbols that have an identical or similar meaning for mankind generally."

44. Ibid.

45. There is, of course, a strong tendency in psycho-analytically oriented interpretations of art to see all efficacious symbols as archetypal in character, even if they are only transparent to "deep probing" and often highly imaginative speculation.

46. And thus someone like Donald Keene can state (but possibly somewhat overstate) that "A Nō play like Matsukaze...means almost exactly to us what it must have meant to the Japanese of the fourteenth century." 20 Plays of the Nō Theatre (New York: Columbia University Press, 1970), p. 3. Zeami himself cautioned us in this regard when writing: "Among those who witness Nō plays, the connoisseurs see with their minds, while the untutored see with their eyes. What the mind sees is the essence; what the eyes see is the performance." "The Book of the Way of the Highest Flower," trans. by Donald Keene in Sources of Japanese Tradition, compiled by Ryusaku Tsunoda, Wm. Theodore de Bary and Donald Keene (New York: Columbia University Press, 1958), p. 302.

47. See Stuart Hampshire, "Logic and Appreciation," in Problems in Aesthetics, edited by Morris Weitz (London: The Macmillan Company, 1959), p. 823. where he notes that "things are (in a sense) recognized before they are really seen or heard. 'What does it mean?' is the primitive reaction which prevents [aesthetic] perception."

48. Richard Wollheim, Art and Its Objects (New York: Harper & Row Publishers, 1968), pp. 127-28.

49. See, for example, Max Loehr, "Art-Historical Art: Ching Painting," Oriental Art, Vol. 16, no. 1 (Spring 1970).

CONCLUSIONS

Comparative aesthetics, as I understand it, is not simply a descriptive, cross-cultural, meta-aesthetics--a comparing of one set of aesthetic concepts with another from some presumed cultural-free perspective. It is rather an analysis and evaluative interpretation of aesthetic concepts from cultures other than one's own for the sake of enriching one's basic philosophic understanding of art and the aesthetic experience of art-works--East or West.

From our analysis of some aspects of the theory of *rasa* we conclude that the essential aesthetic quality of our experience of art-works is neither subjective nor objective, insofar as the aesthetic process cannot be spatialized adequately and must rather be understood as an active participation of a knowing, informed experiencer of an object that controls the experience of it. To experience an art-work properly, which is to say in the fullness of its own authentic being, requires on the part of the experiencer a sensitivity disciplined through knowledge; for an art-work doesn't so much express a personal emotion which can be just naively responded to, as it does an "impersonal" emotion-complex that is rooted solidly in everyone's experience but which is "purified" and thereby made essential. This understanding of "expression" makes possible the preservation of the autonomy of art while at the same time it relates art closely to life. It insists that art is sui generis, that works of art give rise to new and distinctive emotions and insights; and that art is grounded in a common life experience from which it can never properly be sundered. It also enables us to see the differences between aesthetic experience and pure spiritual or religious experience, for aesthetic experience, unlike pure spiritual experience, is always of an aesthetic object, an art-work, that controls the experience of it. A work of art is not a means to a non-aesthetic state, but precisely to an aesthetic apprehension, which apprehension, when fully realized, is nevertheless spiritual in character.

The analysis of yūgen, in connection with the experience of the famous Rock Garden at Ryōanji, shows that the concept of beauty in art need not be confined to the terms in which, in Western aesthetics, it is usually dealt with; on the contrary, the analysis shows that beauty may be understood not as a quality of an art object (or just some subjective state of a viewer), but as the aesthetic presence of the art-work itself as the work is apprehended by one who is knowingly open to it. Beauty is the essential being of the art-work as the art-work is available to disciplined sensitivity.

An analysis of the possibilities of comparative criticism corrects, however, what might appear to be a one-sided "essentialist" interpretation of art, by concluding that an art-work is a multi-dimensional and many leveled object of meaning (as well as value) and that to experience an art-work as it is in its own being one must apprehend it as an individual thing with a meaning in its culture. We must, in other words, reach the work of art in its essential being as a meaning and value in and through its various dimensions of aesthetic relevance, no matter how complex they may be. The essentially aesthetic object, the art-work has a concentrated vitality and meaning, is attained properly only as a unique object in a culture--for that is what the work of art itself is.

BIBLIOGRAPHY

An excellent and quite comprehensive bibliography of Western aesthetics may be found in Frank A. Tillman and Steven M. Cahn's Philosophy of Art and Aesthetics: From Plato to Wittgenstein (New York: Harper & Row, 1969), pp. 745 ff. Among the histories of aesthetics listed there K. E. Gilbert and H. Kuhn's A History of Aesthetics is especially recommended.

A rather vast literature on the arts of Asia is now available in English and in other Western languages; a literature that has been written mainly by art historians and critics and which is, accordingly, concerned primarily with tracing the development and distinctive characteristics of different schools and styles of art and with the work of individual artists. The following bibliographic selection of Asian materials represents a list of some of those works which are concerned to a considerable extent with fundamental aesthetic principles and problems.

Indian

    Chaudhury, P. J. "Catharsis in the Light of Indian Aesthetics," the Journal of Art and Art Criticism, XV, 2 (December 1956).
    Coomaraswamy, Ananda K. The Dance of Shiva. New York: The Noonday Press, 1957.

_____. The Transformation of Nature in Art.
New York: Dover Publications, 1956.

Dasgupta, S. N. Fundamentals of Indian Art.
Bombay: Bharatiya Vidya Bhavan, 1960.

De, S. K. Sanskrit Poetics as a Study of Aesthetic. Berkeley and Los Angeles: University of California Press, 1963.

Gerow, Edwin and Ashok Aklujkar. "On Śānta Rasa in Sanskrit Poetics," Journal of the American Oriental Society, 92, 1 (January-March 1972).

Gnoli, Raniero. The Aesthetic Experience according to Abhinavagupta. Varanasi: The Chowkhamba Sanskrit Series Office, 1968.

Hiriyanna, M. Art Experience. Mysore: Kavyalaya Publishers, 1954.

Honeywell, J. A. "The Poetic Theory of Viśvanātha," The Journal of Aesthetics and Art Criticism, XXVIII, 2 (Winter 1969).

Mahadevan, T. M. P. The Philosophy of Beauty. Bombay: Bharatiya Vidya Bhavan, 1969.

Masson, J. L. and M. V. Patwardhan. Śāntarasa and Abhinavagupta's Philosophy of Aesthetics. Poona: Bhandarkar Oriental Research Institute, 1969.

Pandy, K. C. Abhinavagupta: An Historical and Philosophical Study. Varanasi: The Chowkhamba Sanskrit Series Office, 2nd edition, 1963.

_____. Comparative Aesthetics. Vol. I Indian Aesthetics. Varanasi: The Chowkhamba Sanskrit Series Office, 1959.

Raghavan, V. The Number of Rasas. Adyar: The Adyar Library, 1940.

Thampi, G. B. Mohan. "'Rasa' as Aesthetic Experience," The Journal of Aesthetics and Art Criticism, XXIV, 1, pt. 1 (Fall 1965).

Zimmer, Heinrich. Myths and Symbols in Indian Art and Civilization. Edited by Joseph Campbell. New York: Harper & Brothers, 1962.

_____. The Arts of Indian Asia. Completed and edited by Joseph Campbell. Bollingen Series XXXIX. 2 vols. New York: Pantheon Books, 1955.

Japanese

Fukuda, Rikutaro, et al. Proceedings of the International Round Table On the Relations Between Japanese and Western Arts. Tokyo: Japanese National Commission for UNESCO, 1969.

Japanese Classics Translation Committee, Nippon Gakujutsu Shinkōkai. The Noh Drama. Tokyo and Rutland: Charles E. Tuttle Company, 1955.

Keene, Donald. "Japanese Aesthetics," Philosophy East and West, XIX, 3 (July 1969).

_____, ed. 20 Plays of the Nō Theatre. New York and London: Columbia University Press, 1970.

Lancaster, Clay. "Metaphysical Beliefs and Architectural Principles," The Journal of Aesthetics and Art Criticism, XIV, 2 (March 1956).

Nakamura, Hajime. Ways of Thinking of Eastern Peoples: India, China, Tibet, Japan, edited by Philip P. Wiener. Honolulu: East-West Center Press, 1964.

Pronko, Leonard Cabell. *Theatre East and West*. Berkeley and Los Angeles: University of California Press, 1967.

Sansom, G. B. *Japan: A Short Cultural History*. Revised edition. New York: Appleton-Century-Crofts, Inc., 1945.

Shigemori, Kanto. *Japanese Gardens.* Tokyo: Japan Publications, Inc., 1971.

Sieffert, René. *La tradition secrète du NÔ*. Paris: Gallimard, 1960.

Tsunoda, Ryusaku, Wm. Theodore de Bary and Donald Keene, compilers. *Sources of Japanese Tradition*. New York: Columbia University Press, 1958. Chapts. IX, XIV, XIX.

Ueda, Makoto. *Literary and Art Theories in Japan*. Cleveland: The Press of Western Reserve University, 1967.

Waley, Arthur. *The No Plays of Japan*. New York: Grove Press, 1957.

Warner, Langdon. *The Enduring Art of Japan*. Cambridge: Harvard University Press, 1952.

Chinese

Acker, William R. B. *Some T'ang and Pre-t'ang Texts on Chinese Painting*. Leiden: E. J. Brill, 1954.

Binyon, Lawrence. *Chinese Art*. London: Kegan, Paul, Trench, Trubner & Co. Ltd., 1935.

Bush, Susan. *The Chinese Literati on Painting*. Harvard-Yenching Institute Studies, XXVII, 1971.

Cahill, James. *Chinese Painting*. Lausanne: Editions d'Art Albert Skira, 1960.

_____. "Confucian Elements in the Theory of Painting," in *The Confucian Persuasion,* edited by Arthur F. Wright. Stanford: Stanford University Press, 1960.

_____. "The Six Laws and How to Read Them," *Ars Orientalis*, IV, 1961.

Chang, Chung-yuan. *Creativity and Taoism: A Study of Chinese Philosophy, Art and Poetry.* New York: The Julian Press, Inc., 1963.

Contag, Victoria. *Chinese Masters of the 17th Century*, trans. by Michael Bullock. London: Lund Humphries, 1969.

_____. "The Unique Characteristics of Chinese Landscapes Pictures," *Chinese Art Society of America*, III, 1952.

Fong, Wen. "On Hsieh Ho's 'Liu-fa'," *Oriental Art*, IX, 4 (Winter 1963).

Fry, Roger, et al. *Chinese Art: An Introductory Review of Painting, Ceramics, Textiles, Bronzes, Sculpture, Jade, etc.* Burlington Magazine Monographs. London: Bote Batsford, Ltd., 1925.

Gulik, R. H. van. *Chinese Pictorial Art As Viewed by the Connoisseur.* Rome: Instituto Italiano per il Medio ed Estremo Oriente, 1958.

Loehr, Max. *Chinese Painting After Sung.* Yale Art Gallery, Ryerson Lecture, March 2, 1967.

_____. "The Question of Individualism in Chinese Art," *Journal of the History of Ideas*, XII, 2 (1961).

March, Benjamin. "Linear Perspective in Chinese Painting," *Eastern Art*, III. Philadelphia, 1933.

_____. *Some Technical Terms of Chinese Paint-*

ting. American Council of Learned Societies Studies in Chinese and Related Civilizations, no. 2. Baltimore: Waverly Press, Inc., 1935.

Mungello, David. "Neo-Confucianism and Wen-Jen Aesthetic Theory," *Philosophy East and West*, XIX, 4 (October 1969).

Rowley, George. *Principles of Chinese Painting*. Princeton: Princeton University Press, 1959.

Sakanishi, Shio, trans. *An Essay on Landscape Painting by Kuo Hsi*. London: John Murray, 1935.

_____, trans. *The Spirit of the Brush: Being the Outlook of Chinese Painters on Nature from Eastern Chin to Five Dynasties, A.D. 317-960*. London: John Murray, 1939.

Sickman, Lawrence, et al. *Chinese Calligraphy and Painting in the Collection of John M. Crawford, Jr.* New York: The Pierpoint Morgan Library, 1962.

_____ and Alexander Soper. *The Art and Architecture of China*. Baltimore: Penguin Books, Inc., 1956.

Sirén, Osvald. *Chinese Painting: Leading Masters and Principles*. 7 vols. New York: The Ronald Press, 1956-58.

_____. *The Chinese on the Art of Painting*. New York: Schocken Books, 1963.

Soper, Alexander. "Standards of Quality in Norther Sung Painting," *Archives of the Chinese Art Society of America*, XI, 1957.

Sullivan, Michael. *A Short History of Chinese Art*. Berkeley and Los Angeles: University of California Press, 1967.